❧ Love Unveiled ❧

A COLLECTION OF POETRY

2001 - 2008

Written by

WILLIAM G. FERGUSON

COVER PHOTOGRAPHY by Ashley Ferguson

Photo taken March 2008 "Pacific Ocean Sunset"

*The poetry that is presented in this book is original poetry

It has been collected through the years of 2000 – 2008.

The author's website is www.loveunveiled.ca
"Poet for Hire" is a "personalized" poetry service for special occasions
that the author offers on his site.

Order this book online at www.trafford.com
or email orders@trafford.com

Most Trafford titles are also available at major online book retailers.

Note for Librarians: A cataloguing record for this book is available from Library
and Archives Canada at www.collectionscanada.ca/amicus/index-e.html

Printed in Victoria, BC, Canada.

ISBN: 978-1-4251-9029-3 (soft)
ISBN: 978-1-4251-9030-9 (hard)
ISBN: 978-1-4251-9031-6 (ebook)

*Our mission is to efficiently provide the world's finest, most comprehensive
book publishing service, enabling every author to experience success.
To find out how to publish your book, your way, and have it available
worldwide, visit us online at www.trafford.com*

Trafford rev. 8/13/2009

 www.trafford.com

North America & international
toll-free: 1 888 232 4444 (USA & Canada)
phone: 250 383 6864 ♦ fax: 812 355 4082

FORWARD

I'm quite sure that at some point in your life, you have experienced more than one of the emotions that I've attempted to put into words in this collection of poetry. For anyone who knows me personally or has been a piece of the love and life puzzles that follow, whether a good piece or a bad one, a large piece or a small one, I want you to know that what I have written over the course of my years is in no way an attempt to embarrass you, me, or anyone; nor to devalue our past experiences. It is merely the recollection of it all and the accounting of it all through my poetry.

Our search for true love can be long and tedious and my poems reflect that fact. Love is a non-exact science and therefore, accountability for its disasters should be forgivable offences. I have forgiven all of the offences against me and hope only for the same in return.

For those who don't know me, I hope that my experiences may mirror some of their own and offer some sort of good out of it all. I wish that all aspects of romance could hold up to our expectations and that all relationships stood the tests of time, however, that would be impossible. Both the difficulty of locating and the challenges of maintaining this very unique and special relationship, are the very traits that make it so desirable for us all!

To those who have made their relationships work and have stood together through thick and thin, I say sincerely, Congratulations! I hope that all of the years that you have spent together have been happy ones! I admire your courage and your perseverance! You have attained what we all so desperately desire; you have beaten the odds that are so squarely against you both.

*To Anne and William Q. who celebrated 61 years together before his passing, you are truly an inspiration for us all and as your son, I have always been extremely proud of you both!

*To Joanne and Norbert who will soon celebrate their 35'th Wedding Anniversary, the very best of life and love for what will undoubtedly be the rest of your days, together!

Though I have, thus far, not fared as well as you all, I maintain my optimism!

Despite what I may have been labelled on occasion, I consider myself to be a gentleman through and through. I adore women, I appreciate women and I revere women. I'm a loving and loyal partner, having never lied or cheated, nor ever entertained the idea.

I know that growing up in a stable and loving home has instilled in me the expectations that I have for my own relationships. I have always felt that there is something more to it than I have been lucky enough to find, or rather unlucky enough not to have.

I wanted the magic but I got the circus; I wanted the passion but got the drama. I've reached out for warmth and ended up cuddled to an ice cube; I put my heart and my soul into a commitment, but after many years found myself having to start out all over again when it fell apart painfully and unexpectedly. I take my part willingly in that blame.

The more we face failure in our search, the colder we can become. The hardest part is not so much keeping the desire burning inside of ourselves, but finding another who is as willing and as able as us to do the same. It can't happen without commitment and trust. I'm certainly not the only person on this Earth that has lived this roller coaster ride we call love. The romantic follies of my young adult years became far more serious as those years slipped away. Suddenly and dramatically there was a need for the search to take a far more honest approach. There was a deep desire in me for the closeness and the trust of a truly loving partnership. The problem was that this dream became harder and harder to bring to reality. No matter how diligently I tried, I still felt emptiness and discontent in my heart. I often wondered if I had ever really been in love at all before, or if I ever would be in the future. I questioned whether I was even capable of feeling and sharing love at all!

One of the constants in my life has been the ability to put my thoughts into words in the form of poetry. It was a gift from my Grandmother I believe, who was a remarkable poet. As long as I can remember I have been writing poems; from the age of seven or eight onwards. I have also been somewhat of a romantic fellow; an emotional sort who believes in the fairy tale that we all find our soul mate and live happily forever. I'm not saying that it can't happen; I'm only saying that it is taking its sweet time coming to me.

I hope that my poetry may touch you through its joy more-so than its sorrow. All of our relationships have their good points as well as their bad. It's hard sometimes to remember and to honour the good ones when they can be so easily outweighed by the bad, but for the sake of our future interests, it's a necessity to try and do so. I also hope that my poetry can remind you of times past, highlight times present and give hope for those times yet to come. Love is a shaky roller coaster ride at best; it is however, here, there and everywhere and is an emotion that must be reckoned with, rather than turned away from.

Even in a failed effort, love etches and imprints into our hearts, the joy and the excitement of its wondrous beginnings. Hopefully it has given us reason to seek it again, but this time, on our own terms and with our own expectations as the rules of engagement! Eventually, we learn not to settle for any less. We just can't afford to do it anymore. Love is an education that we all learn one step at a time; a lesson that we need to remember well!

Love Explained

I've often heard it described,
As a state of total bliss;
A sudden sweet euphoria,
That begins with just a kiss.

It lingers from a distance,
Preparing for its strike.
It spreads its manic venom,
With just one single bite.

You lose your self control,
To the power of its ways.
It defies all common logic,
And it traps you in a maze.

I've heard some people say,
That it brings them happiness.
It brightens every single day,
That they stand up to its tests.

It can bring the best of times,
And calm your restless soul;
Or it can hurt you to no end,
Then discard you in the cold.

It takes lots of extra effort,
From two, to make it work;
But the failures of just one,
To turn those hopes to hurt.

You open your heart to trust;
You give it all you've got.
You pray you won't be crushed,
By the heartache it can cause.

Step past those times of doubt,
With swift and hopeful strides.
Work your worries inside out,
And clear them from your mind.

There is never worse a feeling,
Than a love that falls apart.
It tears your life to pieces,
And it violates your heart.

Take stock in what it offers;
Keep it tightly in your grasp.
Fight to hold it all together,
With the will to make it last.

Your hard work will afford you,
Someone special in your life.
A partner to support you;
One to make it all worthwhile.

Love is what we make it,
Though we never understand.
If we don't try to embrace it,
It slides right through our hands.

When it tests our strength,
We find we must decide;
To fight to try and save it,
Or to run and try to hide?

We love for many reasons,
Yet we fail for many more.
We regret our poor decisions,
But must face what lies in store.

We lose our trust at times;
We struggle with our pains;
But to pass up on that chance,
Would be not to love again.

Love is what you're seeking;
Try hard to see it through.
You'll find it out there waiting;
Reserved for only you!

There are many shapes and forms that love takes on in our lives; many different types of love that we may experience; the love of our children, our families and our friends; love of life itself and the things we do that make us feel alive and well. There is also love and faith in our spiritual beliefs and for some sad souls, there is overwhelming love of self. The greatest and most challenging love however, is the love that keeps couples together through the years. This is the love that we all crave if we are indeed serious about love at all. This is "true love" and it is the hardest love that we will ever have to search for in our lives! Sadly, the search may last a lifetime and for some, yield no success.

All of these forms of love make up part of the variety that it offers to us, should we be lucky enough, patient enough and trusting enough not only to find them, but to hold on to them as tightly as we can. In a simplified attempt of defining love, I would have to say that it is the offering of our affections and our hearts and souls to other people or to other interests in life, in the hopes that our actions bring back to us an honest, respectful and fair return for our efforts.

Throughout the course of our lives, we encounter the opportunity to love and to be loved in return. For the very few, the love that they find is a healthy and genuinely shared love that can endure the tests of time and grow stronger all of the days that they live. It's that magical fairy tale ending that we all pray for, but very few of us find. It's two people that have that connection; that chemistry; that honest resolve to work things out through the worst of times and to share happily together the best of times.

For some of us however, through the failures of love lost, this joyous accomplishment seems forever out of our reach. It's a search that sometimes steals our dignity, robs us of our self worth and breaks our will to trust again. It takes a long time to put the hurt behind and to break out of the shell that love lost can encapsulate us in. Sometimes we re-live every bad event of the experience over and over in our minds in the hopes that we can release ourselves of the guilt and lay the blame squarely elsewhere; sometimes we just lay the blame without any deep thought. No-one is ever completely free of blame despite their insistence and there is always at least two sides to every story.

We seek love out despite the pain and the heartache that our search and the failures of our efforts quite often cause us. Like moths to a bright light, we are drawn to the gratification of kind words spoken; a hug when in doubt; knowing there is someone who cares for us as we care for them. We long for closeness, for passion and excitement; for the security of trusting and being trusted in return.

In most cases, from the moment we enter this earth we are cared for, nurtured, protected and shown affection from our parent(s). This feeling of kindness and warmth is bred into our expectations. As we grow apart from the security of our youth, our hope is to duplicate that safety and security and to add the trust and passion and the strength and unity that we have been directed to expect.

We put our hearts out to others, excited by one form of initial attraction or another and hopeful that it's a shared attraction that we both are entertaining. In that moment, we are unmasking our vulnerability and though still guarded, we are placing our most revered and most secretive intentions on the table to be dissected and either accepted or refused.

Perhaps others have not had the same kind of upbringing that we have. They have been shown no love in their youth to carry with them into the relationships they enter. They've been abused, demoralized, degraded and left to fend for themselves. They've seen parents quit and walk away with no regard for the feelings or the welfare of the families that they leave behind. They, in turn, manipulate the love that they are offered in the same way that they have witnessed it being manipulated in the past.

Honest and sincere love is not possible with these kinds of people. There is no future for us in this type of relationship no matter how we try to change them. No matter how hard we try to find the good, this love is destined to fail. With that failure, sometimes comes great pain and abuse both emotionally and sadly, all too often physically. In some cases, there seems to be no escape. We are coerced into believing that it is our faults; that we are worthless and will not survive without them to regulate and manipulate our thoughts and our feelings. These people thrive on control and we are the ones that are controlled. They butcher our self esteem in order to make us dependant on them. They don't have the courage to face those stronger than themselves or smarter than themselves, so they find our weakest flaws and magnify them until we are broken by it.

Though not all failed relationships fit this pattern, this is the ultimate failure. This is the result of not ending soon enough, what has no right to be carried on. It takes great courage to walk away, but when courage has been depleted from us, it's hard to muster it again. If anyone that reads this book, is in that kind of relationship, just get out. Get help and get out right away! No matter what happens; no matter what your partner tries to do to keep you there, leave and don't ever go back! Life will get better, but you need to take the first step.

Love is a basic human desire; a need that we all feel and we all try to fulfill. The poems that follow are of the experiences that I have endured. There is happiness within them; there is great sadness as well. There is excitement and there is anguish; there is regret and there is also momentary disregard. They may touch you in their joy, they may join you in your sorrow.

Just remember that there is always hope...

Nothing is eternal and nothing is written in stone......

True love can and will eventually prevail!

Please enjoy...

Colour Me

Colour me red for my heartbeat;
It beats it's rhythm for you.
Colour me yellow for the suns heat;
It warms me like you do!

Colour me blue like the swirling ocean,
And your beautiful eyes.
Colour me green; my intense devotion,
Drives me crazy sometimes.

Colour me black; when I close my eyes,
I hold you tightly in my mind.
Colour me grey; in the morning light,
I wake up alone, one more time.

Colour me white; the dress I plan,
To someday see you wear.
Colour me blonde; holding in my hands,
Your lovely silken hair.

Colour me pink; I want you so much,
I need to feel your love.
Colour me orange, for my fiery touch;
You will forever have enough.

Colour me all of the colours of the rainbow.
Colour my life with the sweet things you say.
I will colour you in the only way I know;
I'll give you all of my love each day.

Spiders Web

A moth will always fly to the light,
To the security that it thinks is there.
A bright beacon that shines in the night;
A place of comfort in a dark despair.

The spider builds his trap closely by,
Knowing what nature has always said;
The weak never watch where they fly;
They see the light but not the web.

Life is full of little surprises for us all,
When we mess up and let down our guard.
So many traps; so many tragic ways to fall,
Leaving heartbreak and deepened scars.

Love is an accident waiting to happen;
We tend to disregard our common sense.
We sacrifice security for the want of being happy,
And we suffer for our efforts in the end.

We place our hearts on our sleeves,
Trusting that our lovers will do the same.
Sometimes we are brutally deceived;
Played like pawns in a pre-meditated game.

Why do we bother going back for more,
When we know that the odds are against?
We see our hearts stomped on the floor,
But we think we may still have a chance.

We fly to the light; we crave the warmth;
We block the sorrow out of our heads.
To have known love once is to want it more;
The light heals the wounds we have bled.

Like those weak and starry eyed moths,
We know the dangers, but choose instead;
To risk the pain and the inevitable cost,
Of being caught again in the same old web.

Love Is

It begins with a curiosity;
An attraction that won't go away.
It explodes with a wild ferocity,
When we nurture it day by day.

It starts with the glance of an eye,
A connection in the form of a smile;
That wonderful feeling of butterflies;
And the anticipation that drives us wild.

An offer of friendship is declared,
In the fashion of how it should be;
Knowing that more may soon be shared,
But the steps must come naturally.

It's going to bed alone every night,
And seeing her eyes in your mind.
Wanting only to see the daylight,
To be with her one more time.

It's finding the pathway together,
And choosing the turns as a team.
Holding hands and walking forever,
Directly into your wildest dreams.

It's sharing the bad with the good,
And fighting to make it through;
Staying together as partners should,
Knowing it's the right thing to do.

It's a wonderful thing to share,
Having someone inside of your heart;
Knowing that they will be there,
Forever, until death do you part.

Another Life - Another Time

You are the soft breeze,
That kisses my face,
And calms my tired mind.

You are the willow tree,
That swings and sways,
With the rhythm of rhyme.

You are the mighty ocean,
That knows no bounds;
A constant, now and forever;

My hearts sweet devotion;
You keep me grounded,
As I piece my life back together.

You are the morning dew,
Making my world glitter,
When the sun starts to rise.

You are the light of the moon,
Making everything brighter,
On the darkest of my nights.

You are my hopes and dreams,
Giving me something nice,
To look forward to each day.

You are a soft running stream,
Trickling from my lonely eyes,
While I sit patiently and wait.

You are my wonderful future,
Perhaps also my past,
From another life, another time.

We are bound together,
So that our love will outlast,
Any other love that we find.

We are destined to be!
How I wish then, was now;
I wish you were here to stay.

One day soon I will see,
Your sweet face in the crowd,
And we will be together again.

My Heart Belongs to You

It may be bruised and damaged;
It might have beaten for so long.
It may be ripped and ravaged;
The subject of a million songs;
But my heart belongs to you!

It may have fallen once or twice,
To another that crossed its path.
Love can sometimes not be nice,
So destiny has brought it back,
Because my heart belongs to you!

I offer it to you in deepest trust,
This lonely cavern, sad yet strong.
Please do with it what you must,
But I hope you'll let it tag along,
Because my heart belongs to you!

I feel your warmth from miles away;
The tenderness of your touch.
I hope to hold your heart someday,
But until then I will have to trust,
That my heart belongs to you!

Our Life Story

In your eyes I see the sunshine;
In your heart, a roaring stream.
I see nature in your lovely soul!

I hope one day you may be mine,
So every lonely day, I dream,
You are in my life for evermore.

In your words I hear the wind;
The warm breath of a summer breeze,
Touching my lips with a sweet kiss.

I don't know where to begin,
To tell you how much it means,
That you help me feel like this.

In your smile I see an oasis,
In the middle of a parched earth;
A reward for the proper path I chose.

I see a treasure in a sea of empty faces;
A pleasure in a world full of hurt;
A sweet scent that tickles my nose.

In our love I see a happy ending;
The fruition of the seeds we planted,
And the harvest we have earned.

Two lovers tired of pretending;
Taking each others lonely hands,
Despite our different worlds.

Growing together, becoming one;
Laughing our way through this life;
Keeping alive that wondrous spark.

Ending life together as it was begun;
Hand in hand and forever side by side;
Our legacy, the true love in our hearts.

Fully and Completely

To love someone fully and completely,
Is to share their joys and their sorrows;
It is to put your faith in their destiny.

To know someone, is to study deeply,
Their yesterdays and their tomorrows;
What has been and what may never be.

To call a feeling love and hold it as true;
To feel the joy and passion it can bring,
You must let it breathe as it grows.

The only way to see this union through,
Is to trust your heart, even when it stings,
And keep your emotions, steady as they go.

If it was meant to be, it always will.
Give it time to find the path it needs,
Or you will forever wander all alone.

Love is gentle and kind, but it can kill.
Life is cruel when your heart bleeds,
Due to flaws you have been shown.

To love someone fully and completely,
You have to understand how they feel,
No matter what you feel inside yourself.

To help that love develop slowly and sweetly;
Trust that the dreams they have are real,
And be patient that things will soon be well.

The Rivers Journey

The river carries on, following its banks,
As my heart sinks deeper inside.
The crashing and thrashing whitewash,
Make it appear a million miles wide.

Rocks protrude, nearly scraping the sky;
Dangers of the path I have endured.
They cut me deeply as I tumble by;
I have been gouged by them all, I'm sure.

Thundering waves muffle my screams,
As my heart cries out for inner peace.
I'm silenced by the anger of this river;
Tormented by the terrors that lay beneath.

Drowning in this river of tears I have cried,
Bobbing on the waves like a dead branch;
Too tired to fight as emptiness fills my eyes;
Resigning my fortune to very little chance.

Clinging to an old log that passes my way;
It keeps my head from sinking below.
Somehow I find the courage to pray;
I ask for help from an old Friend I know.

I find the strength; the will to survive,
Through the wisdom of His words.
The promises He makes, opens my eyes;
I gather my courage now, re-assured.

There is no quick escape it would seem;
This raging river must be seen to its end.
I can make it out alive, wherever it leads,
And be strong enough to start over again.

Love is seen as a sweet running brook,
But discontent can make waters run deep.
It offers suspense, like a best selling book;
But can be spiteful if it lulls you to sleep.

Love is a violent, raging torrent of hate,
Kept at bay with patience and great care.
Under control it can light up your days,
And fill with happiness, those who share.

It can bring two people together for life,
If they work side by side for a common goal.
It can make families of husbands and wives,
Through the fusing of their hearts and souls.

A ferocious beast sits within loves' bounds,
Waiting patiently for its chance to attack.
Love can create the ugliest monster around;
It's almost impossible to be driven back.

It can rip helpless families into tiny shreds,
With one slash from its mighty claws.
It can turn dreams into nightmares instead,
And turn gains into painful losses.

Love can turn peace into fear and mistrust,
Fuelled by doubts and petty jealousies.
It can open the door to dishonesty and lust,
Destroying our promises of monogamy.

When all is lost, your life is over it seems;
Love has crippled you and left you for dead.
It will toss your limp body into this river,
And you will float beside me to the end.

Just remember that there is always hope;
This river of tears must lead somewhere.
Healing can happen if we harness the ghosts,
And show the monster that we really do care.

Pray to your Friend to be guided through,
The twists and turns; the jagged rocks.
With a lot of hard work, what we set out to do,
Can re-kindle the love that's been lost.

The Proposal

I missed you all day,
I hope that you know.
I keep thinking of you,
Wherever I go.

I miss talking to you,
When you aren't around.
That voice that you do;
That sweet sexy sound.

I miss how you tell me,
To eat better food.
I know that you care;
I don't think it's rude.

I love when you say,
That you miss me too.
It makes me feel loved,
When you say that you do.

I hope that you'll stay,
In my heart and my soul.
You warm up the blood,
That once ran so cold.

I wouldn't go far,
Without you in my life.
I would constantly smile,
If you'd just be my wife.

I hope you'll consider,
What I so sincerely request.
Our lives, spent together,
Would be simply the best.

Give me your hand;
Hold me close to your heart.
What God puts together,
Let no man take apart!

Lazy Day

When we wake in the morning,
I will pull you close to me,
And tell you that I love you even more.

Then, without any warning,
I will whisper to you sweetly,
That I am happier than ever before.

I will look into your eyes,
And touch my fingers to your cheek;
I'll run them softly through your hair.

In that moment, I will realize,
There is nowhere that I'd rather be,
Than in that warm bed that we share.

The world can go to Hell today!
They can all chase their own tails;
They will survive without you and me.

We can stay and make love all day,
Safe and snug behind these four walls,
We can do anything that we please.

There is nothing, nor will there ever be,
A love like you and I will always share;
This love that we have built together.

Every moment that you are here with me,
I will show you how much I really care;
This lazy day will keep us here forever.

Until the End of Time

Will we be ok you ask me?
Yes my love we will be fine!
We will be together laughing,
Until the end of time!

Until the end of time I will be there for you,
Sharing all the joys that life can give.

Until the end of time I will grow with you;
We will be closer every day that we live.

Until the end of time I will hold your heart,
As closely to my own heart as you let me.

Until the end of time I will fan that spark,
While it grows into the flame of our destiny.

Until the end of time I will make love to you,
With the passion of a man that's possessed.

Until the end of time I will stay forever true;
We will both know we are truly blessed.

Until the end of time I will make you laugh;
I'll keep a huge smile on your pretty face.

Until the end of time you'll be my better half,
And I wouldn't have it any other way.

Until the end of time I am yours my love;
Take my heart and hold it closely to your own.

Until the end of time is never long enough;
You're my hopes, my dreams and my home!

Will we be ok you ask me?
Yes my love, we will be fine!
We will spend our days laughing,
Until the end of time!

Questions

When push comes to shove and the pressure is on,
Will you stay there in love or will you move on?
When the clock on the wall says it's time to decide;
When the chips start to fall will you stand up and fight?

Will you run to your lover or will you just turn the page?
Will you seek out another while consumed by your rage?
Can you look in the mirror and swear that you tried,
Or did you bow to your fears, running somewhere to hide?

Can you hold out your heart and feel what is there,
Or let it all fall apart and pretend you don't care?
When love takes a turn through a path of mistrust,
Will it destroy you inside or will you be strong enough?

Love Anticipated and Desired:

There is nothing more exciting than the anticipation of a new chance for love; be it from directly in front of us, or even from a long distance. It puts a certain quickness in our step and a silly smile on our faces. It gives us hope for the future and even though we realize that we have been through this before and have the scars to show for it, we hold on tightly to those dreams.

In this world of ever changing technology, there is no limit geographically to where love can eventually find us. The internet is becoming the norm in the dating world and must be taken very seriously. With that medium comes a different kind of love. It offers us the chance to be in love from a distance and the safety of screening our possible partners in an effort to catch a lie or a familiarity that raises a red flag in our minds. It also gives us the ability to be anonymous and to be able to change or delete the relationship with the click of a mouse. Love, like everything else in the world changes with the times. Though it will always be the same feeling and the same emotion, the way that it presents its opportunities to us has changed dramatically!

Some of us bear that difficult quality of being shy when it comes to expressing our feeling to others. We keep inside what we pray we could release. Sometimes we play games with those that we are attracted to, simply because we are afraid to let them in on the fact that we are interested in them. We crave affection, but fear rejection. Better to have lost the opportunity to get close to someone than to be hurt by them, or to be made fun of for our efforts to be honest. We self destruct and walk away in the belief that we never had a chance in the first place.

How many of those opportunities could have given us the "true love" that we sought? How close we are, but yet, how far we stay away!

Happiness can walk directly into our path, but if we are afraid of it, we will never recognise it. It can tap us on the shoulder but if we turn away nervously, it will mistake our fear for rejection and then seek out another.

Love is a game of odds; a fortune of luck, whether it be good luck or bad. Love can only be found if we march towards it with optimism, although optimism is so much easier from a safe distance. When we meet someone that we desire, we have to summon the courage to let them know. We can watch from a distance, but only long enough to gather the strength to give it a try. Love may just surprise us when we least expect it to!

Sweet Love

My sweet love, let me hold you to me;
Let me kiss your soft lips.
My sweet love, take my hand and be free,
Of these shackles and whips.

My lovely flower let me make love with you,
So we can melt into one.
Once again every hour, a sweet passion so true,
Our journey's begun.

Darling, my whole being longs for your touch;
It begs for your embrace.
Be together with me; explode a rhythm of love,
And a rainbow of taste.

Hold me forever in the spot in your heart,
That waits for me now.
I promise to never let our love come apart,
Anywhere, anyhow.

My far away lover, divided by the times,
And the miles between.
I will search for no other, for your heart is all mine,
On this nineteen inch screen!

An Online Plea

What is it that I want to say,
How can I put this all across?
I was happily in love one day,
But in time it all was lost.

That was many years ago,
But you never forget the thrill!
Moving forward, you always know,
That if you can again, you will!

Here I am on this silly internet,
Trying to find that special soul.
Though it hasn't happened as of yet,
I will keep my dreams on hold.

So
If you are kind and self assured;
If you see life with a smile.
I'd love to meet and share some words,
For just a little while.

If you are sweet and full of life,
And not full of yourself.
I'd love to gaze into your eyes;
I'm sure it would go well!

If you are looking for a gentleman,
Who will treat you with respect;
A warm heart who understands,
Then we should try to connect.

If you have time in your busy life,
For a man who loves to share;
Write to me please, right away;
We'll take it right from there!

If you love poems and songs,
That tell you how I really feel;
Pretty flowers when I'm wrong,
And an honest heart that's real;

If you love romance every day,
And closeness in the night.
A guy who'll never run away,
But would rather love than fight;

Just say hello, or email back,
To this message so sincere.
Before this sad life hurries past,
I'd love to have you here!

Silence Prevails

That moment when I first see you,
I will look into your beautiful eyes;
Then you will have my heart!

When our hands first touch they will clasp,
Knowing inside that they belong;
Knowing they were meant to be entwined.

When we kiss we will draw together closer.
Our lips and tongues will explore,
Until they are tangled and familiar.

When we first make love together,
It will be a journey that we have only dreamed;
One that knows no beginning and no end!

We will build what it is that we seek.
Working together, one tiny pebble at a time,
We will leave no stone unturned.

We will learn all about one another;
The smiles, the frowns, the anticipations.
We will treasure forever the time that we have!

We will find in each other, ourselves!
We will share our days and our nights,
And endure the loneliness when we are apart.

I pray that we will find,
That which has drawn us so close together.
I would love to fall in love with you!

I would love for you to fall in love with me,
But it won't happen until the time,
That I have the courage to speak these words!

Confusion

My heart is confused about you;
Just when you start falling,
Your insecurities come calling,
And I don't know what to do.

These little messages you send,
Confuse me time after time;
Playing little tricks on my mind,
To which there seems no end.

I want to show you my thoughts.
Want to tell you how much I care,
About the moments we share,
But for the risk of it all being lost.

I wish you'd open up and ignite;
We have so much we could share,
If you would only let me in there.
The sparks would light up our lives.

I don't want to scare you away,
But I really think we could be,
A perfect match, you and me.
I feel that way more every day.

If you are struggling with doubts,
Then I will give you that space,
In hopes that they will erase,
And we can eventually work it out.

It's hard to sit back and watch,
One who is so deeply confused;
One who is afraid of being used,
To the point that it may all be lost.

My Butterfly

A beautiful butterfly,
Floated by on a breeze;
It turned my way and smiled!

It came so close by,
Within reach of me,
That I could see into its eyes.

I reached out my hand,
To bring it closer to me,
Being careful not to scare it away.

It did not understand,
That I wanted it to be,
On my hand every single day.

It flew to my fingers,
And settled right there,
With a smile I will never outgrow.

The longer it lingered,
The more we would share;
The more that I wanted to know.

I stroked its soft wings,
With the gentlest of touch,
And the passion dictated the rest.

We talked about things,
Until the dawn from the dusk;
When I awoke, my butterfly had left.

I went back to that place,
Wanting to see it again,
To ask why it had chosen to leave.

I could see in its face,
That it flew in the pain,
Of once having been deceived.

It had found a new chance,
To fly in the breeze;
It had learned to enjoy the sights.

So far away were my plans,
From the freedom it needs,
I realized it wouldn't be right.

I'll watch her fly free,
Like a bird, born again,
Not expecting she'll ever roost.

She is beautiful to me,
But I can't hold out my hand;
I know there would be no use.

Perhaps in a short while,
She will tire of the flight,
And the dangers that fill the air.

I will be there to smile;
To look in those eyes,
And tell her how much I still care.

In the Movies

So many thoughts in my head,
My mind is in a constant whirl.
It's playing out like a romantic movie.

As the story comes to an end,
Could I be the guy who gets the girl?
What a sweet ending that would be!

It would be a wondrous beginning,
As the cast of characters is rolled,
And the movie turns to real life.

We would both be there grinning,
Holding each others hearts and souls,
And each others bodies so tight!

So many emotions in my heart;
All of them staggered and stumbling,
Along the path leading to your love.

I knew it right from the very start;
I was nervous and always bumbling,
Because I wanted yours so much.

So many days ahead to know you;
So much for us to share together,
If you would have me by your side.

So many things I'd like to show you,
On our journey towards forever;
So many reasons for us to smile!

Let that movie play out on the screen;
We both will have the lead roles,
And we will be lovers in the end.

We'll fall more in love with every scene,
And when the final curtain unfolds,
We will be both lovers and friends.

Maybe....

I have been watching you for a while,
Struggling just to make ends meet.
You always seem to have a smile,
Whenever I pass you on the street.

The loneliness must be just terrible;
The difficulty of raising a child alone.
The heartbreak must seem unbearable,
These many years now on your own.

You have made it past the pain,
And you've found peace on your own.
You've made the most of every single day,
And given your son a wonderful home.

I never thought that I would ever know,
The sadness that you must have felt.
But suddenly here I am alone and lonely,
Trying to raise two children myself.

I always wondered how anyone could cope,
Facing life with no-one at their side;
Losing their security and most of their hope,
But clinging tightly to their pride.

I pray that I can handle this as well as you;
My children need a loving, helping hand.
I need someone kind to help me too;
Someone like you who can understand.

I hope that I find the nerve to talk to you;
I'd like to get to know you as a friend.
Maybe we could help each other through,
This loneliness that seems to have no end.

For Me and You

With those eyes, such a pretty day;
I can look so deeply into them.
Such a smile, it takes me far away;
I can forget my troubles when,
I look at you.

That sweetness, I have never seen;
Sitting there across from me.
A moment I have only dreamed,
May soon be a reality.
Could it be true?

To know so little about you now,
But loving what I can see;
I want to tell you soon, somehow,
How perfect things could be,
For me and you.

The Summer fades fast outside,
And the wind begins to swirl,
But I'm cozy because in my mind,
Lives a very special girl,
Who'll see it through!

The days pass slowly, waiting for,
A chance to hug and say hello.
My heart is waiting by the door,
Until it's time to go,
To see you.

I hope to find the courage there,
To tell you how I feel.
I have so much I'd like to share:
My hopes, my life, my dreams,
And my truths.

Sometimes I'm just a bit afraid,
To feel this way so fast.
Like you, I'm scared of all the pain,
That's happened in our pasts.
Do you feel it too?

I guess the safest thing to say,
Is that only time will show.
We can take it forward day by day,
And see how far our feelings go;
Just me and you.

A Distant Love

What we are and what we are to be,
Is something that only time can say.
If I am to you, what you are to me,
Love will help us find the way.

Feelings are either stored inside,
Or shared between two who care.
The truth is told and lovers should never lie,
Even when feelings must be spared.

Hearts can beat to different tunes,
As long as the rhythms can blend.
Let me be me and I'll let you be you;
We can share our love as best friends.

We can't change what was never ours,
We have to be accepting at times.
It takes time to heal the multitude of scars,
That past loves have left behind.

Love is emotion, so let it all out;
It needs to speak to be understood.
Passions are stirred by relieving doubts;
Love is bad things that grow into good.

Come to me when you feel it's right;
Let me share my days with you.
I'm here to love you with all my might,
And my love is most certainly true.

Dream with me about those great things,
That we can do together in this life.
Hear the songs that I try hard to sing;
Treasure the words that I try to write.

Come to me when you can my girl,
With open and accepting arms.
Close this distance and share my world;
Find your spot right here in my heart.

You Already Have my Heart

I love it when we talk;
So much I want to say.
So much I need to hear;
Long are these lonely days.

I love it when you smile,
I can see it from the East.
I can feel it in my heart;
It warms me from beneath.

I live to hear your voice,
To hear you say my name.
To kiss the lips that say it,
Before I go insane!

I long to touch your hair,
And whisper in your ear;
To hold you tightly to me,
And take away your fears.

I may not be a warrior,
But I've battled once or twice.
I'm nowhere near a saviour,
But I'll keep you safe all night!

I'm not an Einstein either,
But I know my way around.
I'm not a body builder,
But I'll never let you down!

I'm just a normal guy,
And what I'm telling you is true.
You already have my heart;
One day I'll have yours too!

The First Time

I dream of how it will feel;
The excitement and the passion,
When we first make love.

These dreams are very real;
Being with you is so relaxing,
That I can never get enough.

I dream of seeing in your eyes,
That spark that fires the magic,
When we are so close together.

I feel comfort as I realize,
That our pasts, so sad and tragic,
Could be set aside forever!

I love the touch of your hand,
The feel of your soft skin,
And the tenderness of your kiss.

I long to know and to understand,
The wonderful woman you are within,
And the closeness we've both missed.

I want to become a part of you,
In that passionate, sharing way,
That heightens our relationship.

Share our bodies as lovers do,
And become one, on that day,
When we both are ready for it.

When we make love for the first time,
The sky rockets will be flying high,
And every part of us will be on fire!

We will light together in our minds,
That spark that twinkles in our eyes,
And burns our bodies with desire!

Someone Special like You

Every day the sun rises on us,
And shines its hope in our eyes;
Leaving yesterday's dilemmas,
In the dark shadows behind.

Every morning is a new beginning,
Like a fresh kick at the can.
It's an opportunity to start winning,
Placed squarely in our hands.

Every ray of sunlight is a dream,
To be gathered up and locked away.
When life is not what it should be,
Unlock the dream and take it out to play.

Every time you wake from your sleep,
Thank your God for another chance.
Life is sour but it can also be sweet;
The power of laughter is in your hands.

Easier said than done, I know it well;
Listen to your own advice, that's true!
My days can be nothing but pure Hell;
I'm sure the same applies to you.

But something about that morning sun,
Puts it all into a proper sort of light.
Yesterdays troubles are dead and gone,
And the future is looking very bright!

Forgive me if I let off a little steam;
I'm glad you care enough to listen.
Tell me truthfully you believe in me;
It's the news that I've been missing.

Know that there is power in emotion;
That there is wisdom in curiosity.
There is also trust in true devotion,
That should dispel this negativity.

Know that you are my morning;
Your smile holds the power of the sun.
Though I don't have you here, with me,
I know inside that you are the one.

Try to understand where I'm from;
How I got to where I am right now.
Where most would have turned and run,
It's something my heart would not allow.

Help me find that special feeling;
That love that has eluded me all of my life.
Forgive my moods and my insecurities;
I promise you that things will be alright!

I won't dwell on my troubles or my doubts;
I'll let the sunshine take them all away.
They're my problem and I'll work them out,
Because today is a beautiful new day!

So much more to be happy for than sad;
You hear it said, and it's so true!
I smile when I think of all the fun I have,
Loving someone special like you!

Lady on my Wall

Lovely lady, hanging on that nail,
If you could, would you,
Join me for an ale?

Silent lady, dressed in black;
I hold the key, to set you free,
And to bring your smile back!

Dismal lady, trapped within a frame;
What artist stole your living role,
And took away your name?

Lonely lady, living in your gloom;
I know your pain, mine is the same;
Yet you brighten up this room!

Gypsy lady, captured without your smile;
Did you know, your frown would show,
And last so long a while?

Piercing eyes, staring into my soul;
Do you see, the tortured man in me,
While watching me grow old?

Friend of mine, when others never come;
A painted tear, on cheeks so dear,
That never seems to run.

Youthful lady, what stories you would tell;
You've seen me fall and lose it all,
As you've shared my private Hell.

If I could paint, I'd dress you in colours bright;
I'd sketch a smile, that stretched a mile,
And soothed our lonely nights.

If I could dance, I'd take your lovely hand;
I'd hold you tight with all my might,
Until we couldn't stand!

I'd sing a song, and promise you my life;
I'd break that painters curse, with every verse,
And make our worlds alright!

Lifeless lady, still you pose without me;
A foolish dream, that seems obscene,
Of what we both could be.

Stay my lady, keep your spot another while;
When I'm gone, you'll struggle on;
I hope someday you'll smile!

Lovely lady, hanging on a nail;
If you could, would you,
Join me for an ale?

Soul Mate

I have walked the perimeter of these endless wars,
Looking for my lost mate; in a love that will never end.
A thousand times, pacing endlessly back and forth;
Wading blindly through the spilled blood of my friends.

I have felt the deadly bullets singe my golden hair;
Fired from the lifeless ghosts, as I passed them by.
I've snorted the stench of death that lingers in the air,
And kneeled with women and children as they cried.

I have sought you out through these many centuries,
Coming so close, I could almost feel your gentle touch.
I've reached for you with arms that remained empty;
So close to your sweet kiss, but yet, never close enough.

Every time that I find you, you are taken away from me;
Stolen from the sidelines of a tragic battle I must fight.
I can't keep you safe from these ruthless enemies,
So I lay them down one by one, to face the night.

In the morning when the sweet sun rises once again,
I walk the battlefield waiting for you to finally run to me.
With tears in my eyes and drying blood on my hands;
My soul mate; my timeless love, you are nowhere to be seen.

I am a soldier, compelled to protect the weaker masses,
But I am a man as well, and wanting just to stop and rest.
To watch a flower sprout proudly through bloodied ashes;
To lay my head softly and forever on your beating chest.

I am a lover, kept at bay by the fortunes of this crazy fight.
A mercenary bound forever by my name to wear these scars.
My soul mate stands waiting, ready for time to finally right,
These wrongs mankind has bargained that keep us apart.

Given the Chance

It's hard to contain my smile;
My heart has been filled with life.
My hopes have been met in style,
And the world seems suddenly right.

My worries have been neatly discarded,
By the words that I heard you say.
That pain that was tearing me apart,
Has been soothed and washed away.

When you told me that you loved me,
And that you wanted me by your side,
I was happier than any man could be;
I can still feel the excitement in my mind!

I want to make you happy every day;
I will be the man that you depend on.
I want to be a part of you, in every way,
And to comfort you if things go wrong.

We can share our days in splendour,
If we hold tight and give it one good try.
If we trust deeply in each other,
We will find love at each others side.

Thank you for giving me the chance,
To be your hearts one and only desire!
Today I truly am a lucky man;
My life is full of joy, my heart is on fire!

Net Meeting

As I sit here, writing this poem for you,
I want to know what's in your head;
Every thought, every action, every dream.

I wonder if you are wondering too,
About my thoughts and what I've said;
What I feel and what you mean to me?

As I sit here missing you another day,
In front of my computer when we talk;
I wonder what it would be like to kiss.

So close in heart, but so far away;
Sharing time through this infernal box;
How can one you've never met, be missed?

I care less about what others may think,
I know inside that we share a bond,
And when we speak, we speak the truth.

I know that if I turned around and blinked,
You would not suddenly be gone.
If I shut out the world, I would not lose you.

I don't care about these damn insecurities,
I forget them in your printed out smile,
And have buried them all in a hole far away.

A sweet distanced love is a love of purity;
There are no lies that will fill in the miles,
And no cruel deception that lies in wait.

My heart is yours; it's warm and waiting,
For that moment when you will come to me,
And collect the love that waits in store.

Until that day, I will keep on contemplating,
How special it is that we both believe,
We can find happiness forevermore.

I will sit here wondering what you are doing;
What thoughts are in your mind today,
And how lucky I am to have ever met you.

Thinking of you as I sit here enjoying,
The hopes that you are in my life to stay,
And the desire to make it all come true.

Love Found:

To think that *"this"* finally may be the *"one"*

Your heart beats to a different rhythm; your knees wobble and all logic gets tossed out the window! The pain and the battles of the past seem to fade in our memories as we hope and pray for the fresh possibilities of that one basic human desire…to be loved and respected in return!

Despite what this new adventure holds in store for us, we enter it in a cautious but ever optimistic approach. How silly we must look to others, walking in a daze, hand in hand; barely aware yet of who we are even dating, but clinging to the excitement that our hearts are pumping into our minds through our touch.

We are past the thinking, the weighing of pros and cons. We have gone for it and are now in the first pages of what we hope will be a long and well written love story. Certainly the fears are still ripe in our minds; the failures and the pains of past experiences gone badly have not disappeared, but have been put on hold somewhere in the back of our heads. We truly hope that we are being accepted and romanced for what will be the long run, not the short one. For now, we are blinded by the power and the euphoria of the emotion.

Where others may judge our actions and the actions of our new partners, they don't know what it is that we have found inside of each other, though we may only be pretending that we do. We are quick to defend this interaction of our hearts; to justify to others that we have made the right choice in pursuing this joining. Why do we feel the need to explain our actions? It's really none of their damn business! Their negativity is an anchor on our optimism, their interventions a cancer to the wellness of our emotions.

Perhaps the loneliness or perhaps our needs and our desires are throwing us back into the fates of love, but regardless, we are there now. We have committed to the opportunity that has presented itself to us. We are blinded by our hopes and we pray that we can stay that way. We are shielded from the pains of the past by a thin wall of excitement.

Should that wall thicken, we may just have a chance, but if it disintegrates we are doomed to the same failures that we have endured before. Without a pleasant deviation, the circle will only continue its turbulent turn. Without an effort, we will never break the cycle. We will forever remain on the outside looking in, with wonder and sadness for our state.

This is the point where patience and understanding are most needed...
...in the very beginning!

An Angel

I really do believe in angels now;
In case you're wondering how,
It's because I've met one.

She takes my sad heart to a place,
With one little look on her face,
That I never want to come back from.

I believe in true love for a change;
She has helped me re-arrange,
The sad emotions I've been feeling.

She has opened my sleepy eyes,
To a fresh and wonderful surprise;
That has my senses all reeling!

She is floating above me, waiting;
Worried of the risk she may be taking,
But wanting to land in my ragged life.

Her sweet smile is mesmerizing;
I stare longingly at the far horizon,
Hoping someday she may be my wife.

Careful I must be, not to frighten her.
Patiently I will wait until she is sure;
I stand here with my arms open wide.

If she chooses to spend time with me,
I can't tell you how happy I would be,
To dry the sadness from my eyes.

So strong is this flowering emotion;
So powerful the focus of my devotion;
So hard to wait for Spring to bloom.

I cling on every word she tells me,
Hoping my attentions won't dispel me!
Have I told her that I love her, too soon?

This angel that I welcome in my heart,
Could fulfill me, or could tear me apart;
Have I constructed this love all by myself?

She's the future, or she'll be part of my past.
Am I too late or am I too fast?
I suppose that now, only time will tell.

Far From Home

All through the night, I think of you.
I wonder where and how you are.
I try to stop myself from feeling blue,
But sometimes it's just a bit too hard.

I keep the phone right near my head,
And when it rings, I rush to pick it up.
I hold your pillow closely in my bed;
I smile widely when you start to talk.

If I am driving alone down the highway,
I hold my cell in my other hand.
I wait and wait for it to finally vibrate,
With the text message that you send.

I know your ring, I've told you many times.
I can feel it tickle my heart with its sound.
When you say hello, I want to sing;
It's nice to have your sweet voice around.

I close my eyes and see you on the beach,
Walking along, looking out at the waves.
I wonder if you close your eyes and see me;
Wandering without you all of these days?

Everything I do now, involves part of you;
Every thought I have shows me your smile.
Every lonely moment I think of us as two,
Who will become one, in just a little while!

Every beat of my heart, calls your name;
It reminds me of how much I truly care.
It carries your lovely image to my brain;
You are here, though you still are there.

Soon when I see your sweet face in mine,
And I feel your tender lips on my own.
There will never be regret for wasted time,
Just the joy of finally having you home.

Wake Up

Wake up my love;
Wipe the sleep from your eyes.
The night has been rough,
But has finally passed by.

The stars shared their light,
As you wandered your dreams.
They shone on you brightly,
To light the path back to me.

Wake up my sweet;
Take a deep breath inside.
See me stand at your feet,
With my arms open wide.

See me offer my heart,
With no strings attached.
It's time now to start,
To forget all of the past.

Put your hand in my hand,
And come now with me.
All the things that we planned,
Can now come to be.

Our lives can be shared,
And our love can combine.
Open your heart;
Let it wrap around mine.

Open your mind,
To the things that can be.
The future may wind,
But our path leads to peace.

Gather your courage,
And don't ever stop.
Our love will soon flourish,
The way that we want.

Stand up and fight,
For what you know is the truth.
Our love is in sight,
And my heart is for you.

Your Puppet

Pull me this way, pull me that;
I'm your puppet and I love it.
Keep my strings nice and tight!

Pick me up or leave me flat;
I can never get enough of it.
You make me feel so nice!

How you turn me into mush;
You make me crazy for your heart;
I pray that I'll soon be inside!

How you drive me nuts with lust;
You tear my sanity beyond apart;
You put the puppy dog in my eyes!

How you control my every thought;
As you commandeer my dreams.
How you make me jump so high!

You make me sweat, like all is lost,
When I take things to extremes,
Then make me melt when things are right.

How can you control me so?
Why am I putty in your hands;
What is this hold you have on me?

I'm big and strong but tender though;
You make me feel like Superman,
When you really need me to be.

Damn it girl, don't you know yet,
I'm yours, through and through;
Just come and carry me away.

When I'm silly, don't forget;
I'm so much in love with you,
That you will always get your way.

You wonder why I flip and flop,
But you must know deep inside,
I'll always do what you desire.

You make me want you non-stop;
With a sparkle in my blue eyes;
You make me jump higher and higher.

You're magic baby, don't you know?
I'm a puppet in tangled strings,
But you straighten them all out!

I'll keep on dancing, even though,
It's for you that my heart sings,
And that song will never run out!

Together to the End

Trust me with your heart;
I will keep it safe,
And guard it from the pain.
Trust me with your love,
And someday you'll say,
That you would do it all again.

Trust me with your smile,
And it will always light,
Your sweet and lovely face.
Share with me your style,
And teach me so I might,
Walk beside you at your pace.

Trust me with your secrets,
So we may know each other,
Completely, both inside and out.
Share with me your dreams,
So we can cuddle together,
When the night is in doubt.

Hold my hand in yours,
And walk with me through time,
To that place you want to be.
Share what lies in store,
And as our hearts combine,
Our worries will wander free.

Be my lover and my friend,
Until time is taken away forever,
And we are but memories left behind.
We will dance together to the end,
And then share that day together,
The way we shared our lives.

What We Need

It's funny how things happen,
When you least expect them to.
How your life can change completely,
And your heart can be renewed.

It's something that you hope for,
But then you doubt it ever will.
You've felt it once or twice before,
The sudden passion and the thrill.

Sadly, others haven't felt that way;
They've preyed upon your hopes.
They've lied with every word they say,
And they've made your love a joke.

They've used you for their pleasure,
And cared little for your pain.
They've stolen what you treasure,
Then turned and walked away.

That's what makes you special;
A shiny diamond in my eyes.
More substance than I can measure,
And a sweetness that makes me sigh

Still, you seek that honest man,
That will treat you with respect.
One who will take you by the hand,
And lead you far beyond the rest.

You haven't lost your smile,
Through the troubles in your life.
I hope you'll trust me in a while,
Because I'd like to make it right.

You are a true romantic;
A crazy dreamer just like me;
But is that a disadvantage,
Or does it give us what we need?

Could it be Me

Do you think,
You'd ever like to meet me?
Share a smile; a drink,
And finally get to greet me?

We can spend an hour,
Laughing out loud together.
I'll bring you flowers;
We can talk about the weather.

Do you hope,
To find someone that's caring;
One that's full of silly jokes,
And just a little daring?

Can you picture,
Any kind of chance?
That we can spend forever,
Immersed in sweet romance?

Do you really care?
Does my age deter you?
It's only fair,
To wonder if it does do.

An older man,
Is so much more mature!
Tender loving hands,
And passion in his words.

Do you know,
I'd like to be the one,
Who gets to show,
How life can be so fun.

It's up to you;
On whom my hopes depend.
Do you like me too,
Or will this fantasy soon end?

Waiting for You

My skies would be the bluest of blues;
My oceans a deep shade of green.
My heart would skip a beat or two,
And a thousand more beats in between.

My days would be sunny and sweet;
My nights, so warm and tender.
My dreams would play to eternity;
In the dawn they would not surrender.

The loneliness that empty hearts feel;
The heartbreak of passions denied.
Love can conquer in time if it's real;
It can put a sparkle back in our eyes.

I hope that our hearts can combine,
And that magical spark will ignite!
I can feel the flames here in mine;
I'm fanning them fiercely tonight.

How wonderful to meet you now,
When my hopes of love were fading.
I hope you'll let me show you how,
It's for you, that I've been waiting.

Promises

I don't have lots of money;
Don't drive a fancy car.
Sometimes I'm far from funny,
And I'm no good on guitar.

I can't promise you the moon,
That rock is just too far;
But I can tell you that I love you,
And that I do with all my heart!

I don't have a monstrous castle,
With Picasso's on the wall.
No uniform with giant tassels,
And no gold to wear at all.

I don't look like an Adonis,
Though I feel, someday I may;
I will always make you laugh,
And keep a smile on your face!

I can't give you fancy diamonds,
That blind folks with their glare,
But I will never give up trying,
To show how much I care.

I can't give you a fancy wedding,
The invitations would be few;
Just some family and friends,
And the love I'm offering you.

I can give you sunny mornings;
Warm evenings and safe nights.
I'll make our love be never boring,
And our passions feel so right!

I can promise you, that forever,
I will be there at your side.
I also swear that never,
Shall a teardrop touch your eyes.

You see my love, I may not be,
The most perfect guy around,
But I promise not to ever be,
A weight that drags you down!

It's Late For Love

It's hard to be in love,
When you are the only one;
It's tough to be the first to fall.
When friendship isn't quite enough,
It really isn't lots of fun,
To sit and wait for her to call.

It's hard to let her know,
Exactly how you feel inside,
For fear of scaring her away.
You try not to let it show,
From the sparkle in your eyes,
Or the silly things you say.

You carry on the best you can,
But toss and turn all night,
Wishing you could let her know;
How good it felt to hold her hand,
In the Autumn moonlight,
On the way home from the show.

How you wished it was forever,
But home arrived to soon,
And a kiss would be out of line.
How you longed to be together;
All alone, just the two of you,
In a different place and time.

How you wanted to make love,
So badly that it hurt,
But you couldn't let her know.
How your stomach felt so rough,
To walk away without the girl,
And back to being all alone.

It's hard to fall in love without,
Someone knowing how you feel,
And sharing your desires.
Hopes can soon turn into doubts,
And even though your love is real,
You can call your heart a liar.

Trust me when I tell you,
That love is nothing if not shared,
But a heartache all the way.
Don't ever do what I do;
If you love someone who cares,
Just tell her right away.

Loves Questions

Where will we be, when time tells our tale?
What will we have to show for the journey?
Will we work to survive and fight not to fail,
Or be beaten to death from the worry?

Where will we go when the path is laid out?
Will we follow or will we lead all the way?
How will we conquer our feelings of doubt,
And smile proudly with every new day?

How do you keep a spark burning brightly,
In a world so sad and so terribly cold?
Will we huddle together, near enough to the light,
To keep our hearts warm as we both grow old?

What can we say to each other; to ourselves,
To keep our promises fresh in our minds?
Will we ever get to know each other so well,
That we can leave our insecurities behind?

Time will show us both the proper direction,
As it unravels the mysteries in our lives.
Stay close as it ticks and never lose the attraction,
That we first saw in each others eyes!

Glad You are my Man

I want to sing a song for you,
And watch you as you dance;
I want to see your blue eyes smile.

I want to walk that path with you,
Holding tightly to your hand,
And love you more with every mile.

I want to share my life with you,
As your partner and your lover,
Until the day I leave this earth.

I know inside, you love me too,
And that when we are together,
We will treasure what its worth.

I want to write a poem for you;
The greatest love poem ever,
That will live forever in time;

To show you that I love you,
Like I have never loved another,
And that I want you to be mine.

I want to lay there beside you;
Our minds another world away,
While we catch our breath again.

I want to press my body to you,
And smile proudly as you say,
"I'm so glad you are my man"!

Let Me In

Take me into your life,
Don't let me walk away.
Let me be there every night,
And let me see you every day.

Trust me with your heart,
I would never do you wrong.
I want to do my part,
To help and keep you strong.

Love me like I love you,
Share with me all you feel.
Know inside, my aim is true,
And my desire for you is real.

Let me hold your hand,
While I whisper in your ear;
I want to be that lucky man,
That you keep forever near.

Let me fight the battles,
That make you want to run.
They will not leave you rattled;
I know they can be won.

Don't be afraid off the unknown;
I can take those fears away.
I will never let you be alone,
If you take me in to stay.

I feel you getting closer,
The more you get to know me.
Less and less afraid,
And trying hard to show me.

I feel the spark that you resonate;
The power of your soul;
The confusion as you contemplate,
Opening up that door.

I see your eye in the keyhole,
Analyzing my intentions;
Your hand on the door knob,
Frozen by fears' intervention.

I feel your heart beating,
As I press against the wood.
Love can be so damn defeating;
I'd hold you tightly if I could.

I'm standing here waiting for you,
As the snow falls all around.
I'm here to see this through;
My feet are frozen to the ground.

Let me in my sweet nervous girl;
Let me sit there by the fire.
I'd tackle this entire world,
To help you feel inspired.

I am yours and yours alone,
If want me to be that way.
Together we could build a home,
If you'd just let me in to stay.

It all Takes Time

Put your heart back together boy,
You're way out of line.
Stop talking about forever boy,
You do it all the time.

Don't you know by now it doesn't work that way?
You're acting like a love struck fool!
Love is in every sentence that you say,
And it's breaking all the rules.

Take your time and try to relax boy;
You're in too much of a rush.
Give your head a little shake boy;
All your words have turned to mush.

You can't be in love if you've never met;
You're just lonely and going over the top.
She doesn't know you that well yet;
If you push it, it may all be lost.

Get a grip on some reality boy;
It just doesn't work that way.
You'll end up as a casualty boy,
And your dreams will wash away.

It's okay to offer your heart in your hand,
But don't expect her to grasp it tight.
You can throw it out to see where it lands,
But the choice is hers; she has that right.

Back up and count to ten boy,
Give her some room to breathe.
Stop asking where and when boy,
Just sit back and wait and see.

If she wants you she will come to you,
When her heart is ready to be shared.
She will never love if she's told to;
Forcing her feelings would not be fair.

It takes time to know you well boy,
She can't run to you right away.
Time is the only way to tell boy,
You'll have to take it day by day.

You've shared wonderful times together,
But then again, you shared some that were not.
If you just let things happen, it will get better,
But if you push too hard, it will be lost.

Keep her close and let her know boy,
That she is always in your heart.
Be careful how you show your love boy,
Or you will tear this thing apart.

Special Angel

Have you ever seen an angel?
Have you ever touched her helping hand?
When you were sinking deep in danger,
Did she pull you from the quick sand?

Did you thank her for her kindness?
Did you whisper in her ear;
That although you've lived in blindness,
It's so nice to have her there.

Have you ever kissed an angel,
And held her closely to your heart?
Have you touched her with such passion,
That your fingers gave off sparks?

Did you hold her tightly to you;
Sleep the night with her at your side?
Did you tell her your secrets and your truths,
While you gazed into her eyes?

Did an angel ever spend the night,
And wake you gently at the dawn;
Or did you turn over on your side,
To find that she was gone?

My angel came in my time of need,
And covered my pain with her wings.
She helped me to become what I can be;
She showed me how to sing.

My angel offered me her entire heart,
To do with as I pleased.
She offered me a fresh new start,
And showed me to my dreams.

Have you ever seen an angel,
Just turn around and count to three.
If you want to see an angel,
She's standing here with me!

We Came Together

We came together,
At a time when we both needed;
Though we never,
Thought that it could ever be.

We found each other,
When the odds were dead against;
We laughed together,
No longer needing to pretend.

We took the chance,
And threw all caution to the wind.
A fresh sweet romance,
On the promise of best friends.

We have our pleasures,
So intense and always so fulfilling.
We share our time together;
The ride is nothing short of thrilling!

There are occasional times,
When things don't seem to glide along;
When we feel inside,
That something may be wrong.

We'll work it out,

Like lovers sharing their dreams.

Whenever we are in doubt,

We have to trust and try hard to believe.

The truth is sweetie,

You make me happy every day.

I hope you'll tell me,

That you feel the same way.

Our love is a young one,

But can grow to heights we can't imagine!

Keep your faith strong,

And if in doubt, we need to try and hang on.

As our love grows,

So will the possibilities that it brings;

And God only knows,

The songs our hearts will one day sing!

The past is done with;

I won't hurt you like the others.

The truth of it all, is,

I want to share this life together.

Love Lost:

There is numbing shock, disappointment, anxiety and denial when a love is suddenly lost. For those who take their relationships to heart, it is their worst fears come to life. Though some may just bounce forward and forget the failure, the true romantic is devastated by this change of fortune. Having been together a long time can make it more devastating but the duration of the relationship is not directly relative to the pain. The intensity of the one that gave the most will dictate the extent of the pain in the same. Regardless, it is one of life's most difficult times and the most damaging turn around that anyone need ever face.

Love lost can lead to emotions so far on the other side of the spectrum that they seem unrelated; but they are related. There is shock and denial; there is eventually anger; there is self abuse in some cases and there is ultimately hate. After the initial shock starts to let loose of you, your thoughts turn to questioning why this horrible event ever occurred. The hidden innuendos that we didn't notice when we were blinded by love, crawl to the surface. Why didn't we see them then?

The next step of our emotional repair is the laying of blame. If you are a heartless and unfeeling individual, you can absorb the blame and even laugh about it. If this break up has truly hurt you to no end, then laying the blame hurts you as well, although time will somehow allow you to do it. Generally, you will split the blame; leaving regret for your part, but anger for what has been inflicted upon you. Time turns blame into hate. Hate is the end result of having been deceived, embarrassed, possibly tormented and left all alone to suddenly have to fend for yourself.

They say that time heals all wounds, but in truth, they don't know what they are talking about. Our failures in love are never completely forgotten. The hate will never relent and though it eases over time, it never completely fades. There may be forgiveness and there may be understanding; we may spend years rebuilding our self esteem, but it is never forgotten.

It hurt too much to ever forget; it hurts too much to not remember. Love lost will enter into almost every relationship that we share in the future. It will be our constant reminder that nothing is forever; nothing is guaranteed. Those lucky enough to stay together may not ever experience this horrible happening, but no matter who you are or how strong your relationship is, there is always the doubt. There is always the worry that love may be lost and that your perfect world will come crashing down. Many of those lovers who do not fall apart, perhaps should have. Familiarity breeds contempt. It is better to lose a love than to have to endure a painful one. Love is about happiness, not anger, abuse and pain.

There is Hope Together

We both have a lot to learn,
About one other;
It's normal to wonder aloud.
Learning can sometimes hurt,
When two lovers, together,
Are stubborn and so damn proud.

I have never been in love before,
Despite what you may guess;
These feelings are new to me.
It's such a strange euphoria;
Such a trial of errors and tests;
I want so much to succeed!

There is hope for everyone that cares to try.
There is love for those who refuse to let it die,
And there is hope for both you and me, together.

Open your heart to my passion;
Let it consume you as it does me;
Let it light your darkened eyes.
This is more than infatuation;
If you look hard enough you'll see,
These hopes that will not die.

Come to me and hold me closely;
Feel the blood pump in my veins;
My heart beats for only you.
Let the follies of the past go;
I'm a man who welcomes change,
And one who finally sees the truth.

My love, there is hope for everyone that cares to try;
There is hope for those who are honest and true inside,
And there is great hope for you and me, together.

She Doesn't Love You

Broken pieces on the ground,
With jagged edges all around.
Torn papers on the floor;
Piles of poems that rhyme no more.
She doesn't love you anymore.

Broken heart, it's finally clear,
So turn and face your wildest fear.
Steady stream right down the drain;
Your love lies bleeding once again.
She doesn't love you anymore.

Laughter turns to falling tears;
You've lost a love to last the years.
Words were spoken out of turn;
When will you ever start to learn?
She doesn't love you anymore.

All is lost, sad days return;
You tried but once again got burned.
Dry your eyes and carry on;
The dream is dead, the hope is gone,
Because she doesn't love you anymore.

Old Wounds

I'm very sad that I have to say this;
It breaks my heart to even think it.
You're on your own; you got your wish,
And I'm too tired to do anything but quit.

You took the greatest gift that I could offer;
The re-arranging of my life in the name of love.
I defeated my demons to make myself better,
But you kept telling me that it wasn't enough.

I gave you the freedom that you asked for,
To sort things out and to clear your mind.
I kept our hopes and our dreams together,
And I prayed for you at night while I cried.

I told you I was sorry for what we had become;
Told you that I loved you with all of my soul.
Despite your refusals I still wandered along;
I kept my heart warm though you were so cold.

I sent you flowers just to let you know,
That I was thinking about you every day.
I wrote you poetry so that I could show,
The words you never gave me a chance to say.

I kept the faith; I prayed and I even begged you.
I helped you when you asked me for good advice.
Despite my kindness, the anger inside you grew;
My reflection was pathetic in your cold dead eyes.

If you want your sorry life alone, so be it;
You can spend all of your time hating me.
If you haven't found the kindness to forgive,
Then at least you've found the hatred to be free.

How terribly sad to watch us fall apart;
How bitter and cold to never be given a chance.
How cruel to take a beating, broken heart,
And squeeze the love out with your bare hands.

It took a lot of hard work to make me hurt;
To make me finally give up and walk away.
I hope you find someone to fit your perfect world,
I hope they'll know there's no room for mistakes.

Sit in your lonely world and enjoy yourself;
You have chosen your path for this life.
You've taken my love and sentenced it to Hell,
Without at least giving me a chance to fight.

I'm still here alone, made strong by my faith;
A free bird grounded by a damaged wing.
Weaknesses and injuries get better every day;
Soon, old wounds won't mean a damn thing.

Time will forgive you if it is what you seek.
Everyone is entitled to make a bad choice.
You may find happiness in life without me,
But you didn't need to leave me destroyed.

Three Pails of Coffee

Three pails of coffee and I'm still online,
Searching the net in an effort to find,
Where in the world you are hiding out now.
None of the people finders give me a clue;
My fingers are numb; worn right through.
There must be a way but I can't seem to figure it out.

No longer in Canada and not in the States,
It's like a huge wind storm just blew you away,
From the place that you really do belong.
Our angers exploded in a battle of words,
Too loud for the apologies to even be heard;
Yelling out rights, instead of discussing the wrongs.

It was always that way since the day that we met;
Arguments so fierce that we could never forget,
Let alone find the courage in ourselves to forgive.
Turning our heads so our eyes wouldn't meet;
Both laying there pretending to be fast asleep,
It was a terrible way for us to have to live.

We threw it out to the wolves in the night;
Much better to be alone than to constantly fight,
But loneliness gives you too much time to think.
We should have done better, but we never tried;
We drowned in the pool of tears that we cried;
Resigned ourselves to close our eyes and sink.

Where are you now, I can still see your face,
But I can't find the pathway back to your place;
The maps that I search all read in a hazy blur.
Are you thinking of me as you run and you hide?
If I found your front door would you let me inside?
Would there be any love, I'm really not too sure?

Is your new life so sweet, you don't even miss me?
Do you remember the night that you first kissed me,
And the happiness that we swore we'd both find?
Will we ever meet again and make things right?
Could you please call me now, on this lonely night;
I'm here for you baby, trying to find you online.

Both Love Again

I have written so many poems since you left,
That time has begun to fade the ink.
This flow of emotions, I must truly confess,
Has been clouding the way that I think.

It's true that writers only write when they're sad,
And that love lost is usually the cause.
Their words bare to all, the emotions they have,
And the pains of the love they have lost.

Every line that I've written; I've written for you;
Every word has come from my heart.
Every poem I have sent you speaks only of truth;
How it pains me that we're still apart.

Every day that I wake, I live long in the hopes,
That this is the day that you'll call.
Every night I lay there in my bed all alone,
With enough tears to repaint the walls.

If I had any sense I'd just go on with my life,
And leave these dark days behind.
Time seems to work like a dull rusty knife;
It won't let me cut you out of my mind.

These six months have passed, slower than Hell;
The days seem to stretch until they snap.
With no-one to love, you can't love yourself;
So all you can do is look back.

I'm empty without you; my failures are clear,
but how can a man make amends?
When the woman he loves closes her ears,
And rips up the poems that he sends.

Somehow, some way, this story will close;
The cards will fall where they may.
With or without you, I guess God only knows,
If we'll both love again someday.

Questions

Do you ever think about me,
As you walk your own way?
Do you ever wonder if I'm well?

Did you ever believe in me,
Or the things we would say;
The crazy tales that we would tell.

Don't you wish we could go back,
And start this all over again?
Would we get it right this time?

Find the patience that we lacked,
And do away with the pain,
That cracked our brittle minds.

It's hard to accept that we failed,
When so much time was ahead.
Did we give up too soon?

Why was our love derailed,
Picked apart and left for dead?
Why were our promises ruined?

Did we really try hard enough?
Did we give it all we had?
Why didn't we try to get it back?

Is it too late to save our love?
Have the good times all gone bad?
Is the future now only the past?

I'm willing to give it an honest try,
If you can meet me in the middle.
There is so much more life to live.

Can we look each other in the eyes,
And solve this painful riddle?
Can we both ever learn to forgive?

Dangling on a Thread

So much to gain and so damn much to lose;
Our love dangles on a fraying thread.
So much pain and so little time to choose,
When that line snaps, where will we land?

So blind to the future; so stuck in the past;
When everything good stands before you.
You'd like to be sure but it's too much to ask.
If you wait too long, time may ignore you.

There is no guarantee; the path life will take;
To be alone would be worse than to fail.
The future will be only what you will make,
So you'd better weigh both sides of the scale.

See past the promises and look into the soul;
If you can't trust then try hard to forgive.
Nothing stays warm, left out in the cold,
And being full of hate is no way to live.

Open your mind to the options you hold;
Either work it out or just walk away.
The longer it lingers the more it grows old,
Until that love disappears to stay.

Opening your arms will open your heart;
It will open your mind, your eyes and your ears.
A hug can work magic when you're torn apart;
It can lift you above and beyond your fears.

Our love is begging for a helping hand;
Reach out with all your heart and your soul.
Let those who love you be a part of your plans;
Let me in from this heart numbing cold.

Keep Her Happy

To love is better than not to have,
Even though its passage brings pain.
To share a smile, a tear or a laugh;
A moment kissing in the Summer rain.

To have known the real happiness,
Of having someone truly care for you;
Having someone kinder than the rest;
Someone that will help you get through.

A lover, a partner; your closest friend;
Who looks up to you as their strength.
You would give your life up to defend,
And stretch your heart to any length.

Keep the laughter forever in her eyes;
Let her know exactly how you feel.
Time shadows love and doubts can arise,
That make her wonder if your love is real.

Treat her well; she is there for you.
Make her part of your every thought.
Seek her happiness in all that you do;
Don't take for granted what you've got.

Tell her how much you love her,
When she's not feeling at her best.
Hold her tight and re-assure her;
That you'll always stand up to the test.

You'll never know the pain of losing her,
If you stand strong at her side.
The damage that foolishness can cost you,
Is the poison your love needs, to die.

Trust me when I tell you that it hurts,
To watch your lover walk away;
For the sake of poorly chosen words,
And the use of them by you, in haste.

The Verdict

I don't know what to say,
That hasn't been said before.
It wouldn't do any good,
To say it all once more.

Either you believe it,
Or you never really will.
I have to tell you though,
This feeling really kills.

I never told you any lies;
Never tried to make you sad.
I didn't hope for you to cry,
I gave it all I had.

It's in your hands now,
So take it where you want.
Let my love back in,
Or just leave it and move on.

I have to say, it hurts,
That you haven't any faith.
You question my integrity,
And the promises I've made.

All I wanted was to love you;
To spend time in your heart;
To break down all the barriers,
That keep us miles apart.

So now, do what you must.
I will listen to what you say.
Give me back your trust,
Or just be on your way.

I still love you now,
And have loved you forever;
But I can't give any more,
Unless we are in it together.

I sit here lost in limbo,
Waiting for your axe to fall.
I don't think I deserve it,
But I guess that's not my call.

The Only One

Hard days loom so large, dead ahead;
Tough times and difficult decisions,
With no-one to help ease the burden.
Seeking meaning in the words she said;
Reasoning out this sudden division,
And fighting back, that final curtain.

I really thought that she loved me;
I was sure that she could understand,
But I was completely wrong.
I didn't know that her attention was pity;
That she saw me as a dying man,
And she resented me all along.

If I had known that years before,
I would not have invested my life;
I would not have wasted her time.
If she didn't love me anymore,
Then far before that fateful night,
She should have spoken her mind.

I know my illness killed our plans,
And I know I stopped trying long ago,
But she should have told me the truth.
It was hard to live as half a man,
But how could she ever know,
Unless she walked a mile in my shoes.

I always thought she knew inside,
How frustrating my life had become;
I really thought she understood.
I mourn her now, like she has died;
She felt she couldn't carry on,
And had done the very best she could.

Change of Seasons

I used to sit here and watch the snow fall,
Out this window in front of my computer,
Until it blanketed the ground.
The telephone ready in case you called,
To tell me that you were feeling better,
And you might just come around.

I saw the snow melt and Spring arrive,
While I put my love for you into words,
And practiced what I would say.
But the weather stayed cold in your eyes,
And the words I spoke were never heard,
Though I polished them every day.

Tiny shoots stretching; reaching for the sun,
Through the thaw softened soil overhead;
What beauty may finally sprout?
So many days of promise, that never come.
Our roots bared and laying there, near dead,
In the Spring sunshine, drying out.

Summer brought me out to your garden,
Where you once spent hours with a smile,
When you felt like being alone.
The weeds untouched, the soil hardened,
From no attention in such a long while;
Dying plants strewn amongst the stones.

When the leaves fell and the winds grew cold,
I peered between the frost lines to see,
Your outline outside my window;
But still, I face another Winter all alone.
Time has not brought you home to me,
So as the seasons change, so does my hope.

Outside, the Winter snarls, to let us know,
It's time to light a new fire in our hearths;
Time to gather warm thoughts and prepare.
How much longer can I stay strong, on my own?
There is emptiness inside of my heart;
A love that is crying out to be shared.

Sail On

I stand alone, watching the waves;
Still waiting for you to sail back home.
The others have quit; they've all gone away;
So I continue this vigil on my own.

They all think I'm crazy to stay and wait,
But I know someday you'll sail into sight.
The land I stand on is as firm as my faith,
And my prayers will keep you safe at night.

They tell me that the ocean is far too wide,
And that time can change a travelers plan;
But through the waves of tears I've cried,
I hoped that someday you'd be home again.

Your adventure is now long past due,
We expected you home a long time ago.
You set sail in search of a dream or two,
To find the answers you needed to know.

Your feet have now touched distant lands;
Your eyes have seen cultures unknown.
We've tried our very best to understand;
We've kept a light burning for you at home.

I stand here on the docks waiting for you;
Refusing to give you up to the mighty sea.
My love for you, can only be as true,
As the love you once professed for me.

Sail on, with the winds at your back,
And know that you'll never be alone.
I will be here, clinging tightly to the past,
In case those winds should bring you home.

Hopeless Change

Words spoken in haste, but not really meant,
Only add more fuel to a fire out of control;
Damaging any chance of working out this mess.

Days and nights of sorrows that never end;
Standing here frozen, locked out in the cold,
So deeply sorry but not forgiven of my debt.

Frustration shapes the words that utter loose;
So long a time without any love to hold tight;
So many more months pass, alone and broken.

Apologies and regrets spoken deeply in truth;
Long hard work to change a lost and dying life,
Fuels more laughter with every word spoken.

Emotions dripping through funnels in my brain;
So heavy a price for simply losing my way;
So long a sentence; so bitter these reparations.

From loneliness to resentment, then back again;
A mixture of ups and downs fill these days,
For a life without love yields impatience.

Setting deadlines that are not written in stone;
Only putting more pressure on the two of us;
Simply because they seem to be my last resort.

If only I could help you to see this happy home;
If I could prove to you that I am worth your trust;
If I had the chance to love you just once more.

If you only knew how sorry I am for the past;
How hard I've worked to change the way I am,
And how much you've helped me to find my way.

You'd know why my love for you will always last;
How strong the arm is that offers you its hand;
How much I long to make you happy once again.

The Wait

I am waiting for you my love,
Waiting patiently for your smile.
I haven't seen it now,
In such a long, long while.

I'm lonely for your touch,
I quiver, even at the thought.
I need to feel your embrace,
Before my hopes are lost.

I think of you every moment;
I'm sorry for the past.
I pray you'll someday try,
To forgive and let it pass.

I see you in my dreams,
Your sweet and loving face.
I remember you being here;
Brightening up this place.

We are empty without you,
Rambling along all alone.
We offer our prayers,
Hoping you'll come home.

Your fears are your barrier,
They must be overcome.
I will do my part forever,
To be with you as one.

You were right to walk away,
But only for a time.
To plant the seeds of change,
And open up my mind.

I am a man of learning,
In the lesson you have taught.
Our future could now shine,
So don't let it all be lost.

Take the time that you need,
I will do my penance alone;
But keep an open mind,
And just remember, this is home.

We Need to Learn

She looks at you with sad eyes,
That never ever seem to dry out;
Anger turns to ice in her glare.

She never lets you see her cry,
But inside, you have no doubts;
Despite the facade, she still cares.

You remember back to when you met;
How pretty she was, how alive!
You both were so young and carefree.

It was a time you will never forget,
No matter how hard you must try;
No matter how lonely you will be.

If love can bring two people as one,
It can surely survive a little pain,
To grow again, nurtured through time.

Even if someone should turn and run,
Love can bring them back again,
If they learn to leave the pain behind.

Sometimes we all can lose our way;
Take things for granted a bit too much,
From the bad habits that root in our paths.

Complacency can lead our love astray;
It can compromise our vital trusts,
And tear the whole union into halves.

Our lives are full of twists and turns,
But love is meant to always endure,
No matter the difficulties it may face.

We must be willing to try to learn,
To keep kindness in our every word,
And to think, before we act in haste.

The Girl That Got Away

I took too long;
I messed around,
Playing stupid little games.

I wasn't strong;
I was too proud,
And now you're gone again.

I made you cry,
Because of spite;
I tried to hurt you back.

My stupid lies;
Those crazy fights;
I was so far off track.

I love you still,
Although you're gone;
But that was due to me.

I always will,
Know I was wrong:
I'm sorry, can't you see?

Someday soon,
I'll have the chance,
To fall in love again.

My heart has room,
For sweet romance;
I am a damn good man!

I know I've lost,
The love of my dreams,
To the silly games I played.

Now I feel the cost,
In it's worst extremes,
Of the girl that got away.

The Snow Falls Softly

The snow falls softly to the ground;
I watch it from my window seat,
Thinking only about you.

Its motion steady, without a sound,
Covering up what lays beneath;
The sad and silent truth.

My heart beats a steady dying stream;
Damaged as it has become,
It still holds some hope.

Seeking a spot, still alive and green;
A warm place in the sun;
Your heart is like an icy slope.

Praying for that sun to re-awaken,
And nurture our fallen seed,
From its dormant state.

Remorse for the liberties taken,
And the thoughtless deeds,
That sealed this fate.

The painfully lonely times ahead,
Taunt me both night and day,
Screaming out the cost.

The wounds from which you bled,
Seem to never heal and go away;
And so, our love is lost.

I will await the long coming Spring,
Alone, with only my thoughts of you,
And the cold lifeless snow.

In the hopes your love will sing,
Sweet songs of a trust renewed,
That will awaken that seed to grow.

The snow falls softly to the ground;
I watch it from my window seat,
Thinking only of you.

Love can lead to Hate:

After the mourning and the realization that it's all over and lost, love will show you its other side. How such a wonderful emotion as love can have such a bitter and vengeful edge built into it is truly amazing. When the denial has passed; when the blame has been squarely laid in the most self gratifying location, the ugly side of love emerges.... Hate!

You can talk about forgiveness; you can talk about establishing a wonderful new friendship with a past partner, but it is merely a sweet icing on a very stale cake. We as humans do not forgive deception, nor let go of pain easily and certainly not without harbouring some sort of anger inside. We bottle it forever, into the deepest corner of our subconscious. We release snide quips about our past lovers without even hearing ourselves say them. In any future disagreements with our ex-partners, we are quick to point out their past failures. We're only too happy to pull the most damaging words that we can find in our heads and toss them freely into plain view. It calms us to do so; it's a form of our therapy!

There is nothing as tender on this earth as the human psyche. We retaliate like wounded animals when we are hurt unexpectedly for what we determine to be no reason at all.

When our defence mechanisms kick in, we have ways of dispelling the pain that make it appear as though we have not been as offended as we really have. We laugh about it in the open, only to cry about it in our private moments. Love "gone wrong" multiplies our emotions thousands of times over, causing chaos with our understanding and healing. The last step in the release of these scattered emotions is the acceptance of hate as the final solution. Hate solves a great many problems that a bitter breakup creates.

When we hate, we hate with intensity. It's the last board on a swing bridge that we must cross to get back on the right side of our lives. It's forever the last step that is etched into our hearts and our minds. It's all that we will remember in the future but it is also what propels us towards seeking out love again. Why do we do this to ourselves?

We can't accept failure, even though it was equally our fault. We are wiser and more cautious, which only increases the difficulty of finding love again. There are too many scars for it to be beautiful; too many memories to be clear of mind and too many doubts to be optimistic.

Hate is vindictive and shallow, but it is the only way that we can move forward. It's the bottom end of love; the finality that must be found and applied in order to continue with our lives, our dreams and our expectations of romance and true love.

Just Walk Away

It's not about you any more, you've made your point.
You've changed my world as far as it's going to go.
The blues that you cry have saddened the joint,
But now it's time for me to get on with the show.

You had your reasons, I won't ever deny that.
For a while, it was a terrible way for you to live.
Nothing ever gets solved with a suitcase and hat,
And you're damned if you don't learn to forgive.

To walk away because the times are not well,
Is like quitting when the clouds block a dream.
It's tough for now, but then you never can tell,
Because the best years you haven't yet seen.

You've laid what you blame at my tired feet;
Kicked sand in the eyes that you once lit up.
You hid so well what was buried beneath;
Once it surfaced, you could not make it stop.

Your story never changes; it's a sad tired tale.
Now that book will go back up on the shelf.
You've pinned on me the reasons we failed,
Without taking a good look at yourself.

If it's what you want, it's my last gift to you;
I'm not going to beg you to stay.
Go out on your own, do what you must do,
But don't come back sorry some day.

Famous Lovers

Funny, but you don't mean that much anymore.
I'm so tired of wondering that I've stopped caring.
I've even been caught saying I'll even the score;
I've gone from broken hearted to downright daring!

It's so hard to move onwards and try to forget;
It's ironic when I sit back and try to remember,
The words I thought I would never live to regret;
Turn as cold as a sidewalk in December.

Those evenings of bliss, or whatever we had,
Seem like we took a dagger and drove it into stone.
Both of our hands were embraced on the handle,
But my heart took all the blows, on its own.

I guess it's true, like all the famous lovers say,
You can't stop the pain when love suddenly ends;
But the scars all heal and eventually the hurt goes away,
Leaving hate, as the last reminder of a special friend.

Love is a Game

If you think I may be stressed a bit,
You might just be right.
If you walked my path a day or two,
You'd be just as uptight.

If you think that I don't give a shit,
You might just speak the truth.
I've tried before to sweeten it,
But I've learned it's just no use.

If you think my life is too easy,
Then you're a sad pathetic soul.
You must be close to crazy,
To be so cruel and so damn cold.

Live your life without me;
If there's anything I've learned;
It's that if you try to love me,
You are going to get burned!

I have no heart to give you;
It's all shattered from before.
I have no need to tell the truth,
So don't expect it anymore.

I have no warmth to hold you tight,
No more passion to unveil.
I have no gentle kiss goodnight;
My lips are numb and stale.

All I have is hatred, free and clear;
It has consumed my very soul.
You'd better walk away from here;
My blood is far too cold.

Don't linger in the distance,
Go back to where you came.
Heed closely my insistence;
Because my love is just a game.

Beneath the Surface

On the surface I look to be real;
I smile and I hold my head high.
I try to be honest in the way that I feel,
But deep inside, I just want to die.

I give my heart openly and willingly,
Even though it may not be accepted.
I take my punches hard but politely;
In the manner they are directed.

I assume that when I'm told I'm loved,
It's the truth that my love is offering;
But if that affection is merely a bluff,
I find my own heart soon wavering.

I'm not always as I appear to be;
There's a level of doubt I maintain.
The people that assume they know me,
Think that I easily laugh off the pain.

I happen to be a more sensitive man,
Than what I am usually perceived to be.
I've been hurt before and will be again;
I think it may be my destiny.

I'm not as strong as I let on most days,
I've been known to cry alone.
My heart was warm in so many ways,
But these days, it's as cold as a stone.

On the Shelf

They say that a writer only writes,
When he or she is feeling sad;
When they are contemplating their lives;
The joys and sorrows they have had.

I would have to believe it to be true;
It's the way things are for me.
I started writing the day that I lost you,
Until I filled up a thousand sheets.

The words flowed out like a torrent,
From deep in my heart and my soul.
Every time I tried to ignore it,
The faster and faster they flowed.

I wrote a poem to you every day,
Then I tucked them away in a drawer.
I waited forever, only to hear you say,
That you didn't want me anymore.

How sad these long days have been;
How lonely my life has become.
My poems are filled with empty dreams,
That will never be shared with anyone.

What a waste of a good opportunity,
To work on the problems we shared.
To embrace and declare our unity,
And to prove to each other we care.

To piece back together, a love fallen;
To breathe life in the spoils that lay.
To answer a chance that is calling,
And arise to a brighter new day.

My poems are finished, yet never read;
My love for you, beside them on the shelf.
My heart bleeds from the way you said;
Take your poetry and go to Hell!

The Final Decision

The circle has nearly completed its path;
I am right back to the beginning.
I fought so hard to make this love last;
But surrendered the battles I was winning.

My suffering at the hands of the one I loved,
Has given me the strength to walk away.
To her, my efforts were not near enough;
I have no kind words left in me to say.

The failure lies written on these fading walls;
It will consume my thoughts very soon.
Our love stands destroyed for no reason at all;
Now I'm stranded in this dark empty room.

I'm not sure that I want to feel love again;
She has dulled the softness of my senses.
My heart is broken; bleeding in my hands;
Impaled on the barbs of her cruel defences.

For a problem that could easily be resolved,
With some honest and courageous effort;
A bond is broken and a true love dissolved;
Destroyed by poor intentions forever.

All that is left now is for the word to be said;
Standing tall, I await your instructions.
Breathe in new life, or just leave me for dead,
But be swift with your final decision.

The Turn Around

I can feel that solid wall of ice slowly melt;
The droplets sizzling on my burning heart.
I remember well, how very helpless you felt;
How I turned your love cold from the start.

I know the courage it took you to walk away;
I admire the strength of your convictions.
There was no possible reason for you to stay.
I had to battle myself, my afflictions.

You turned me loose in a world of responsibility,
That for so many years I had denied.
I thought the world owed me for my disability,
So I sat down depressed and waited to die.

Your parting words planted the seeds of change;
Rather than curse you, I took my burden to task.
The most difficult war that any man ever waged;
My heart was broken, but my blood still ran fast.

I'm not saying that my battles have been won;
They will certainly taunt me my whole life long.
If I can survive the fight still alive, yet alone,
Still together, we could have been so strong.

I handled my responsibilities with pride!
I held together a household in deep despair.
I've closed that chapter and opened my eyes,
To the fresh possibilities that wait out there.

It's a long road that I have chosen to wander down;
A road full of deadly pit falls and taunting curves.
I have come a long way but will not turn around;
I'm smarter due to the lessons you've served.

The Shutting of the Door

The words are all spoken;
I wait for your final decision.
The front door is wide open,
And I embrace the new vision.

Won't you come in and play,
This game that I call truth.
Keep your weapons at bay;
In here they have no use.

This is not a house but a home;
It's been one since you departed.
I have rebuilt it on my own;
I always finish what I've started.

In a dark and empty corner,
I make my bed and lay there alone.
I miss the closeness of a partner,
And the comfort that I've known.

If there is any justice in this at all,
I will soon find that special touch.
You could have broken my fall,
But didn't reach out far enough.

Through the open door I can see,
The brick wall that holds you back.
I waited for you to struggle free,
But it had trapped you in the past.

Sad yet optimistic, I move ahead;
And let you slip out of my life.
One turn to gather a fresh new breath,
And the tears in my eyes start to dry.

Remembering your words long ago;
You said time is what will decide.
The winds of time have finally blown;
My door shuts, with you on the outside.

Last Poem

This is the last poem,
That I will write for you.
It's the sad moment,
When I finally know the truth.

The bitter emptiness,
Within my heart.
The biting coldness,
Of our burned out spark.

This is the last time,
I will mention my love.
The very last rhyme,
That my heart will construct.

I'll pack up my poetry,
And wish you the best.
I'll toss this in my files,
Beside all of the rest.

This is the last poem,
I will write for a while.
I must seek out my soul,
And teach it to smile.

I hope you are happy,
In all that you'll be.
I'm okay now knowing,
That it will be without me.

Thoughts on a Snowy Morning

The snow is falling quickly,
Covering the dying grass.
Everywhere I look, it's white!

The streets are all but empty;
Just a ladder of tire tracks,
In the early morning light.

For hours I have watched,
As I sit in this window seat,
Wondering where you are.

Though I know that all is lost,
I wonder if we could ever be,
Back where we once were.

The garden is covered now;
Just a few leaves poking through;
Reaching out for the sun.

I remember once just how,
That garden was part of you,
When we were still one.

All of the memories linger,
But time has a lesson to teach,
As it cleanses the wounded soul.

While we pointed our fingers,
Our dreams slipped out of reach,
And were stranded out in the cold.

The snow covers up the truth;
The saddest of yellows and browns,
That our love became in the end.

So bitter this torment and abuse;
So much anger floating around,
There is no hope to ever be friends.

Let the snow fall, so pretty to see;
Let it bury the pains that I feel,
And shelter me from your words.

In this cold world I am free;
I'm alive and I am real;
The wounds you left no longer hurt.

Sad Poems

I can't keep writing sad poems,
For a love that's near its end.
I mustn't spend these days alone,
I need to find myself a friend.

I shouldn't keep my blinds closed,
While Spring time fills the air.
I'm afraid to let the sadness show,
But I'll try hard not to care.

I've got to put it all past myself,
And move on to what will be.
I've spent too long inside this shell;
I need to finally break free.

Though it may take me a lifetime,
To free myself from your words.
I've got to grasp that lifeline,
And forget what I have heard.

Farther down the line someday,
This will all seem a waste of time.
I've bared my soul in every way,
And let sorrow write my rhymes.

I'm tired of walking on my knees,
Hoping that you might help me rise.
Spring time is calling out to me,
Now that our love has gone and died.

Somewhere in this life I lead,
A true love waits for me to find.
A partner who will set me free,
From the pains love left behind.

My poems will speak of happiness,
And flow forward from my heart.
My feelings will be re-addressed,
As the memories depart.

Buddies

So you want to be friends;
Like buddies you say;
But it's not going to happen;
I just don't feel that way.

You just want to be pals,
But that's not enough.
It's just too hard to shake,
These feelings of love.

You want to be confidants;
We could bet on the game!
We could watch it together,
But it's just not the same.

We could take in a movie,
Or be partners in darts.
There's no way it will work,
It's just not in my heart!

If you want to spend life,
Through both thick and thin,
Then forget those crazy ideas,
And let my love back in.

If you don't hang on to me,
You'll lose me for sure.
I'm in need of a partner,
So your friendship is absurd!

I don't like walking backwards,
Once my foot's in the door;
So find a friend elsewhere,,
We aren't that any more.

Dead and Gone

It's finally over;
Those days were long.
So hard to shoulder,
Right from wrong.

So hard to fight,
For one so cold.
So tough to crack,
A heart of stone.

You're dead and gone;
You're dead and gone.

My pain will cease,
My thoughts, expand.
My heart is free,
To love again.

Prayers unanswered;
So many words.
You had your chances,
But never heard.

You're dead and gone;
You're dead and gone.

This lonely vigil,
Has reached its end.
The deafening signal,
That your hatred sends.
Walk on alone,
And time will tell;
Your journey home,
Will lead straight to Hell.

You're dead and gone,
You're dead and gone.

My love has faded,
It's turned to dust.
My feelings are jaded,
My emotions crushed.

I'll still walk tall,
I'll hold my head high.
I won't ever fall,
And I never will cry.

Because you're dead and gone;
You're dead and gone.

Small Packages

Such clever packaging;
Produced to look so proper; so pleasing to the eye.
So subtly non-distracting;
Concealing all the darkness that lines the walls inside.

An empty container,
Dressed in good intentions and tied in fancy bows.
Hiding the danger,
Of the selfish misdirection that she tries hard not to show.

Her smile is bladed;
See things as she does and you will not be cut to shreds.
Her heart is jagged;
Take her to task and you'll be gutted by its edge.

She suffers delusion;
So poorly done by; her torment is all in her mind.
She lives in confusion;
The hate that she embraces, she fights so hard to find.

Outside of her true heart,
She has nothing to offer but her desire to obtain.
She plays a warm part,
But those with so much have so little left to gain.

She is in it for her;
Unaware that her plans are so simple to see.
She sweetens her words;
She may fool a few but she will never fool me.

I watch her intently,
Openly admiring the ribbons and the little bows.
Her package is empty,
And the top of that box should forever be closed.

Those who know her,
Are bored with the dressing that she displays.
So hard though to tell her,
The friendship I offer her, is wrapped up in hate.

Nobody's Perfect

Tossing and turning in my bed since three;
I'm up now with a coffee in my hand;
Pondering the words that you said to me;
Where they came from, I don't understand!

So easy to hurt someone if you really try;
When they love you, they don't have a chance.
It's childs play to tear them to shreds inside,
And I'm putty in the palm of your hands.

Take my intentions and twist them around,
So they add fuel to the hate that you bare.
Stomp on my heart until it's flat on the ground,
And pretend all the while that you care.

You used to be such a kind and loving person,
But it's hard to remember that, these days.
You had a heart of gold and a head full of reason;
How in the Hell did you lose it this way?

You can focus on my faults and then magnify;
You can spend your time in pursuit of revenge;
But look at yourself; how hard did you try?
How much effort did you honestly spend?

Nobody's perfect, as I'm sure you know now;
People fall into their own private Hells.
The least you could've done was to help me out;
Picked me up once or twice when I fell.

You never once reached out or offered a hand;
You were too busy constructing a stone wall.
The tough times didn't fit easily into your plans,
So you turned and ran away from it all.

I'd wish you the best, but my heart isn't there.
I don't care now if you fall to the ground.
Your words may hurt now, but just be aware;
Sooner or later it will all turn around!

Gunslinger

You've finally put the last bullet in me;
After seeing me plead for my life.
I begged on my knees from the ground,
But you've killed me out of spite.

I hope that you can find some peace,
While you watch my dead corpse rot.
Did the final act give you relief?
Did it exact the revenge that you sought?

When you put a notch in your holster,
It will be all you remember me by.
I hope that your heart can forget,
The look in my sad dying eyes.

Don't go to the trouble of burying me,
Let me fall to pieces in plain view.
When they talk of the fastest shooter,
They will definitely mention you.

I will find my place in the heavens,
And hate you safely from a distance.
I will always wonder why you did it,
But dead men offer no resistance.

Find a partner that shares your views,
But keep your gun close by your side.
People like you who quit on folks,
Leave men in piles, one at a time.

Some day when the trigger turns on you;
And you're standing there in its sights,
Remember the ones that you laid to rest,
And the horrible way that they died.

Take your death as well as those you killed,
When you are captured by the odds.
Save your begging and your sad excuses,
For your meeting with your God.

Love and Life:

Equally as important as the love of others in our lives, is the love of life itself. A person that truly is in love with life is one that sees good in most things that cross his or her path and tries to infuse good into those things that are void of it. You have to be a deep thinking and positive person to find the silver lining in the typical grey clouds that fill our skies. You also have to see hope in others and feel sadness for the suffering that a lot of people must endure in their lives. You have to reach out and help them, in any way that you can.

To see what illness and disease do to good people can be emotionally traumatic to those who truly care. To have it close to your heart and to your home amplifies the pain that is rendered and endured. For all of our strengths, we can be dropped to our knees by disease in seconds, whether it is us that is afflicted, or our friends or family.

When the doctor told me that I had an enlarged heart, caused by the invasion of a virus, the reality of it all hit me like a brick. In much the same fashion as we evolve from loves that we have lost, we also evolve from bad news just like the words that I had heard. There was initial denial, deep remorse and regret and yes, even the anger and the hate! I was angry with the world for taking away my power and my strength in such a cruel manner.

We still have to try and smile though we are in no position to do so, nor are we in the mood. We have to find a positive note to feed off of and enhance our possible recoveries.

Life has so much to offer us; so many wonderful things to reach out and take hold of. How can we give up on it simply because we are facing turmoil within. The beauty of nature; the joy of family and friends and the laughter of our children should demand our full attention. There is no time in this life for feeling sorry for ourselves.

Though my illness contributed to the dismal ending of my marriage; though it changed me into a person that I never expected to be; though it concealed me in a prison of depression; it taught me to never give up. It challenged me to face it head on and beat it to a pulp!

My heart is better now and though I was also diagnosed with skin cancer, my love of life has allowed me to beat both of these illnesses.

I can wake in the morning and look out at a sunny day with the excitement of a child at Christmas. We have to find that excitement in our lives! In order to love anyone, including ourselves, we have to love our lives. We have to be content and positive in what life puts in front of us and make the very best of it…. after all, life is for the living!

Hero

Alone in a terrible nightmare,
That just won't go away.
Scratching at the walls of reality;
They bend, but never break.

Trapped for what seems an eternity now,
And constantly tortured by your fears.
Screaming out at the top of your lungs,
Desperate cries that nobody hears.

Walking a challenging and endless path,
With no direction in your mind.
Each step forward, leaves you two steps back,
And you're running out of time.

Voices that enslave your being;
They tell you how to feel.
People don't seem to understand,
That to you, they seem so real.

Dreams that chase you in your sleep;
A peaceful moment, you long to know.
Sabotaged by this spiteful disease,
And left wandering all alone.

No-one to share your life with now,
But the tormentor of your mind.
No love to spend your nights with;
No earthly comforts for you to find.

Damned for your time on earth;
Victimized by your own thoughts.
There is no cure for this horrible illness;
The scars mark the battles you've fought..

I admire the strength of your conviction;
You are stronger than you care to believe.
To call you sick is a contradiction;
You are a hero to those like me.

My Brother, My Friend

I've always wondered what it's like to be you;
To spend your life with very little hope.
I've wondered what it is that gets you through;
What keeps you strong enough to cope?

I know your pitfall was never of your choosing;
Disease just happens along where it may.
The voices that seem to keep you in confusion;
Will be with you for all of your days.

I know the medications barely do their job;
They sometimes make it all seem worse.
I know it feels as if you were robbed,
And shouldered with this horrific curse.

I see you managing every single day,
Smiling when others would only frown.
The look in your eyes makes me say,
I'm glad you don't let this get you down.

Don't let that smile ever end,
My brother and my friend.

Disease

The first few days are the hardest;
Coming to the realization that you're,
Not as invincible as you once thought.

Your will to fight begins to build,
As you adapt to the new limitations,
Dictated by the disease you've caught.

Regret and self pity take their hold,
When you finally get over the shock,
And begin to face the battles ahead.

Frustration looms nearby, waiting,
For an opportunity to set you straight,
And to settle for good in your head.

So many questions that you can't answer,
Make you wonder forever, why,
Were you the one that was attacked?

With your life shooting upwards,
And so much promise near fruition;
You were finally getting on track.

You remember the stories you read,
About the sadness of it hitting others,
And the way it hits with no warning.

The healthiest of people that unjustly,
Go to sleep in remarkable condition,
But never wake up in the morning.

Time can play tricks on your resolve,
Though you have promised yourself,
That you won't give in without a fight.

If you settle into any acceptance,
Of your disease, as the way it must be,
Then the routine will block out the light.

Days, months and long lost years,
Will pass before you so fast,
That you will lose the will to try.

Anger and futility will boil away,
Inside of you, leaving you cold,
And waiting for the day that you die.

Take it from one who knows,
And has lived the torment you feel;
You are not alone in your pain.

I have been stricken unjustly,
And given up on my dreams,
But have gathered my life together again.

Try to accept this disease,
As a challenge laid before you;
Be the underdog, determined to win.

Live each day for the moment,
And don't fall into any routines,
That allow complacency to kick in.

You are the person that you were before;
Only your lifestyle must change;
Accept it and thank God every day.

One important thing is for sure,
You can still make the most of each day,
If you have the will to find the way.

The Train

The whistle of a train echoes down the line;
  The ground vibrates below my tired feet.
My journey nearly finished; I'm out of time.
  It is destiny that train is mine to finally meet.

The cold steel whines on this bleak Winter day,
  Like the crying of my soul to be released.
So many miles have come and gone my way,
  Too many goals I somehow never reached.

When I was young, I fought against the world;
  I made my own rules and set my own mind.
I was full of energy and as my youth unfurled,
  My friends and family all were left behind.

As a man I was missing love and happiness,
I had grown too self indulged to learn to share.
Days were spent in anger, nights in loneliness;
  There was no-one but myself that even cared.

When time took away the energy that I had,
I was an old man, with an empty wasted heart.
  I regretted the life that left me cold and sad,
  And prayed to my maker for one more start.

Now that my journey is coming to a final end,
I stand here tired, waiting for that train to near;
Without hope, or the comfort of a single friend;
Bold faced, hiding from the torment of my fears.

Where that train will take me, I do not know;
Forgiveness or eternal damnation lays ahead.
While it is true that we reap only what we sow,
Is it ever too late to change the lives we've led?

To A Friend

He was a friendly kind of guy;
Give you the shirt off his back.
His heart was in the right place;
It made up for what he lacked.

His problem was the bottle;
In the end, it did him in.
It robbed him of his health;
A battle he would never win.

He was a friend of mine;
We spent long hours together.
He did a lot of work at my home;
No-one could have done it better.

A carpenter, roofer and a mason;
A jack of all trades kind of guy.
There was nothing he couldn't do,
And nothing he wouldn't try.

His pride was what kept him going;
He knew he was one of the best.
But he never spoke an unkind word,
And he never criticized the rest.

He had it rough in the beginning;
Born into a broke and broken home.
He left it all when he was young,
And went about life on his own.

He learned his skills the tough way;
Through the school of hard knocks.
He showed up every morning though,
And absorbed what he was taught.

He also learned how to drink,
On Fridays when he got paid.
Shared the bottle with his fellow workers;
In construction, that's the way.

He found more solace in the bottle,
Than he'd ever known before.
He said he liked the taste of beer,
And one led to many, many more.

I met him when he was slipping;
The booze had claimed his soul.
It had worn out his willpower,
And it had robbed him of his goals.

I gave him some small jobs,
So at least he could still eat.
But the money that I paid him,
He drank down in defeat.

I gave him clothes to keep him warm;
He was grateful for my help;
But they couldn't keep the cold out,
And so he quickly lost his health.

He spent his last days in bed,
With a bottle in his hand.
No-one came to comfort him;
They just didn't understand.

How could a man with all that talent,
Fall to such a desperate low?
Why did he give in to his demons?
Sometimes, that's just how it goes.

He was rushed into emergency,
And hooked up to life support,
But the doctors in their wisdom,
Had no good news to report.

On the day he finally left us,
He had only his Mother at his side.
She told me that my name,
Was spoken as he died.

The funeral was in the next few days,
But I didn't even attend.
I had done all that I knew how,
To try and save my falling friend.

I regret my actions now,
Wishing that I had been there.
The room was nearly empty,
Because no-one really cared.

Those who once surrounded him,
Pretending to be friends;
Took away his only dignity;
They stole his tools in the end.

His family called me one day,
Asking if he'd left things at my home.
They wanted me to return them,
So they could try and get them sold.

I told them that all he gave me,
Was the comfort of his help!
The kindness that he had inside,
Was something they could never sell.

Buddy, I know you're out there,
Watching the world turn without you.
I want you to know and to remember,
You were one kind and decent dude.

Despite the problems that hurt you,
You were a gentle loving soul.
Take comfort wherever you are now,
With that heart made out of gold!

The Old Man and the Drink

I met him in a tavern;
He bought me one more drink;
Before it touched my lips,
He made me stop and think.

He asked me if I really needed it,
And I wondered why he cared.
He hung his head for a moment,
Then he lifted it and stared.

He told me a story about a kid,
Who had the world in his hands;
A family that really loved him,
And a future in his plans.

When I pressed him for a name,
He sipped his stale, flat beer.
He told me just to shut my mouth,
And to open up my ears.

He talked about the bottle,
And how it can take control;
How it took this man of substance,
And stole away his soul.

The fall, he said, was heavy,
And soon everything was lost.
The hardship of the lesson,
Was the pain of what it cost.

He told his tale of woe,
And he tried to make me see,
Although that man was him,
It might as well be me.

He placed the drink before me,
With one last word of advice.
Just throw this drink away;
Don't let it ruin your life.

When my hand went out,
And grasped that shiny glass,
He watched me tip it to my lips,
And pour it down with a laugh.

He turned and walked away,
With sadness in his eyes.
His wasted stack of words,
Were buried in his sigh.

I cursed him out intensely;
Called him a crazy drunken fool!
I told him not to preach to me,
That I make my own damn rules!

I'll never let it hurt me,
I yelled out as he left!
I'm smarter than you were;
I'm not like all the rest!

He faced me from the open door,
With a smile on his face.
He ordered me a couple more;
Then he laughed and left the place.

Death

Death;
Hiding inside of that dark cloak,
With that sickle by your side;
What fuels your ambitions;
What hides behind your eyes?

What brings you to my place,
With a warrant in your hand?
What makes you so intense,
And such a fear to mortal man?

Death;
What gives you the right,
To call out my name?
To come here in the night,
To steal my soul away?

Show me now, your face;
Let me gaze into your eyes.
Death, I will never go away,
I won't leave with you tonight.

I heard your footsteps creaking,
As you tiptoed down my hall.
I heard my Master speaking,
Telling me I would not fall.

Death;
He told me not to fear you,
Or my soul being pulled away.
He said I could defeat you,
And I would see another day.

He said you weren't His angel;
He said your putrid smell,
Was the earmark of the devil,
And the pit we know as Hell.

He told me to stand tall,
And to send you back your way;
That courage was all I needed,
And that He would give me faith.

Death;
Crawl back into your hole,
You will not feed on me.
The power of my God,
Will keep me alive and free.

Happiness will come,
The day He calls me home.
The evil of your darkness,
Has not, my soul to own.

The promises of heaven,
Will light my journey there;
Where peace and contentment,
Lay in wait for me to share.

To William Q.

Don't leave us Father!
Sometime that day may be;
But it can't be now; I won't allow,
Your tired soul to leave.

Don't let your pains,
Take away your will to live.
You are my friend; don't let it end,
You have so much more to give.

You are that mighty oak,
That towers strongly over us all.
You've lost your leaves but please believe,
That tree will never fall.

I wish that I could say,
We shared together our greatest days.
We both had different interests,
And we went our separate ways.

When I returned you took me in,
And shared my life again.
Not so much as my Father,
But more-so as my friend.

As the child in me slipped away,
And my own began to grow.
I realized that you had been right,
There was so much I didn't know!

You are still my best friend,
And I want you to always be.
Don't leave us now; it's too soon.
I need you here, with me.

The Attic

It's hard sometimes to tidy up;
To sweep away the past;
To throw away the memories,
That we hoped would always last.

Cluttered upstairs in the attic,
Where we've put them to be stored;
In dust covered cardboard boxes;
Hidden behind our attic doors.

Good times, bad times, co-exist;
Joy and laughter, pain and tears;
Reminders of the experiences,
We've collected through the years.

There comes a time in every life,
To open up that long locked door;
To bring our past affairs to order,
From the piles on that dusty floor.

To re-live every happy moment,
And to suffer once again, the pain;
To clean up all of those feelings,
And briefly touch them all again.

Time brings changes to our lives,
As it passes slowly day by day.
Sickness, sadness and even death,
Can steal those memories away.

When all of those memories fade,
And lay forgotten for all of time.
The lessons they should have told,
Are never passed on down the line.

Future generations come and go,
Denied the experience that we held.
Facing the world and on their own,
Without the tales that we could tell.

Keep that attic well organized;
Not just a pile of moments in the dust.
Their hopes and dreams mean a lot,
To those that follow in our trust.

Love Denied

I'm sorry that she didn't stay;
I'm sad that she told me when she left,
She couldn't stand the sight of me.

I'm tormented constantly every day;
Broken hearted at the sudden theft,
Of what I'd hoped our lives could be.

It's a terrible shock when the one you love;
Who has been with you for so long,
Turns her back and walks away.

When she says that you aren't good enough;
She needs to find someone strong,
Because you couldn't keep up anyway.

To be a changed person because of health,
And not only lose your will and desire,
But also to lose the anchor of your soul.

To spend every day in a living Hell;
Tormented by a fierce scorching fire,
And no kind words for you to be consoled.

It's hard to come to the final conclusion,
That someone has given up on you;
That you are not worth the effort to try.

What you thought was love, was just illusion;
You're crushed from learning the truth;
That the love you shared became a lie.

It's devastating to watch someone hurt you,
That you loved with all of your soul;
But all that you get is their hate in return.

You realize that your dreams are all through;
That your heart has been turned out in the cold,
And your feelings have been lit and burned.

So much for forgiveness, it just doesn't exist.
You've been hung for a helpless mistake,
And left dangling on the end of a rope.

For better or for worse, is no longer on the list;
When revenge is the path your lover takes,
And you are gutted and left all alone.

Fight it Now

The hopes turn to worries,
With the words that are heard;
To disbelief, then to fury,
You try and block out the hurt.

The future seems clouded,
If there is a future at all?
What was taken for granted,
Has slammed into a brick wall.

How could it happen to them;
Those who live their lives right.
Be them family or friends,
They are dragged into a fight.

We pray for their welfare,
Like we have never prayed before.
We show them we are still there,
As their curls fall to the floor.

That horrible word cancer,
Takes on a whole new meaning,
When it's us that's in danger,
And our friends who are grieving.

This theft of our freedom;
This stripping of our strength;
Can happen to anyone,
So don't ever try to pretend.

Fight it now, in any way you can,
Before our will starts to weaken.
The answer is in our hands,
And I know, cancer can be beaten!

Bad Word

The door closed like the click of a gun;
The paperwork in his shaking hands.
He had been with me right from day one,
Trying to help me understand.

His eyes shed a tear that rolled down;
Dropping on the results that he held.
There was no escape from the sound,
As it splattered with a deathly yell.

He sat down; a veteran of bad news,
But he stumbled on the words.
He realized then, that I already knew;
Though unspoken it was clearly heard.

I thought about that sweet little boy,
Sitting there alone in the waiting room.
His young life has been so full of joy;
He just wanted me to hurry out soon!

I thought about his future alone,
Without the one constant in his life;
About how what once was a home,
Would soon be so empty inside.

I cursed the God that I once embraced;
I left Him in the examining room behind.
When I looked into my sons smiling face;
God was the farthest thing from my mind.

I'd heard the stories, I'd seen the news,
I'd felt the sadness for those afflicted.
Through the tests, I somehow knew,
What no-one else would have predicted.

Cancer…the word rattled like a snake.
Already bitten, I was lying in the dust;
No second opinion, no quick escape;
Dear God, what will become of us?

I took my boys hand in mine,
Trying to be the same Dad I always was.
I led him from that office, back outside,
Praying my manufactured look was good enough.

I paused at the car, buckling him in;
Caught his eye in mine and I cried.
Where does this explanation best begin?
It just cannot be told with lies.

He looked at me so deeply within;
Dropped his Sponge Bob on the floor;
Then mustered a rugged toothless grin,
That I had never seen before.

He told me that he loved me,
And he knew that I was sad.
He asked how bad can it really be?
And then he told me he was glad.

He was happy that I was so strong,
I was Superman in his eyes.
He said, no matter what was wrong,
He knew we'd be alright.

I held him tightly in my arms,
And kissed him on his rosy cheek.
My son let God back in that car,
And locked out my thoughts of defeat.

I drove to a pizza place nearby,
And we had ourselves a tiny feast.
The strength that boy held inside,
Gave me the courage that I'll need.

I will fight this demon to the end;
Slay it as often as it needs to be;
With the help of my family and friends,
It will never get the best of me.

I will fight with every ounce of strength,
Though my fractured will may weaken.
I will battle it fiercely to any length,
To prove this bad word can be beaten!

No You, No Me

There is no you, no me;
We are all in this together.
There is no escape from destiny,
And no pill to make it better.

There are no secrets known,
To make this go away.
It cuts right to the bone,
No matter what they say.

There is no magic cure;
We haven't come that far.
All there are is words,
That come right from the heart.

A hand offered when we fall,
To lift us back up straight.
A simple telephone call,
When we are feeling the pain.

No one should face it all alone;
Would that be nice if it were you?
Could you sit there in your home,
And survive that awful truth?

Could you fight without an army?
Would you even stand a chance?
Would it not be so disarming,
And the cause of your last stand?

Get up and do your best,
If only to put others at ease.
It can hit you like the rest;
It's a non discriminating disease.

There is no you, no me...
We are all in this together.

Love of Family and Friends:

No greater gift are we given in this life, than family and friends.

Our families are the root of our very existence. We are raised by our parents with love and affection (in most cases) and so we try to raise our own children in that same manner. The changes in the world from the days when we were young, make it difficult most times, but we do our best and hope for the same.

When there is a break up, it is generally the children that take the hardest hit. They love both of their parents, despite what the parents may feel for each other and they only want their families to hold together. It's so hard to be kind to each other when the children are watching, but it's something that must be done. The damage that can be done with words, at that point of a failed relationship is extreme, to say the least.

These days, it's almost as common for the Father to take over the parenting as it is for the Mother. It not only depends on which parent wants to stay more than the other, it also depends on which parent is in a better position to take care of the children. When it comes down to a custody dispute, Fathers are not as poorly done by in the courts as they were for years. I'm a single Father and I know that I did damn well, so never discount the capabilities of a man to care for his children. I do believe though, that there is a genuine need for the influence of both parents on the children, be it from close by, or from a distance. The purpose of a family; a successful family; is for the children to receive and to respect both sexes and to be offered not only the knowledge of both, but also the recognition of the differences between them. Troubles loom in the future if this isn't the way that we raise our kids.

When it comes to our friends, we would hope that they could see past a break up and be civil enough to respect both sides of such a decision. Sadly, that's not usually the case. Friends tend to go to one side or another, either swayed by the separating party or because they are finally able to choose between what was once two but has become a choice. True friends will always be there for you no matter what the predicament.

One way to find out if your friends are true, is to go through bad times and see if they are still there when the smoke clears. Unfortunately, some will not be.

Sprig

A tiny sprig planted in the dirt,
Will grow strong with time.
Tended to and lovingly nurtured,
It will climb like a wild vine.

It will provide happiness,
To the gardener that truly cares.
It will alleviate the loneliness,
Of a garden that was once bare.

In its growth it will give comfort,
To the hands that gave it life.
If it is trimmed and supported,
It will grow full and ripe.

Seldom in this bitter life,
Can you find such a friend.
Through either good or bad times,
Its love for you will never end.

One day it will reach the sky,
No longer a sprig anymore.
It will flower right before your eyes,
And will need your help no more.

You will miss the steady task,
Of caring for it, day by day.
You will realize at long last,
It must fight to find its own way.

When Winter covers its roots,
And it's bent over by the snow.
It will learn the harshest truth,
And will prosper in that growth.

It will straighten to greet the Spring,
And comfort you once again.
It will offer you its seedlings,
And trust them to your loving hands.

When it fades and grows no more,
It will give to you its soul.
To raise its sprigs like before,
And ready them for the coming cold.

Slow Down Boy

Where are you going,
With that head full of dreams?
Slow down and see the truth.

Without even knowing,
Which path you could choose,
You'll only wear out your shoes.

How can you smile,
Like the world is your toy?
You're too young to understand.

A loose carefree style,
Is just fine for a boy,
But not good enough for a man.

Enjoy your short youth,
Before you take on the world;
Live your life as it comes.

Some day the truth,
Will suddenly unfurl,
And tempt you to turn and run.

Stay at your studies,
And learn what you must.
It will help you in the end.

Hang with your buddies,
And keep them in trust;
Everyone needs a friend.

Life can be fun,
But it can also be Hell.
It can totally change overnight.

Once you've begun,
Only time will tell,
If the path that you've chosen is right.

So stay where you are,
For the moment at least.
Get yourself fully prepared.

If you want to go far,
Get the education you need,
Then trust it to take you there!

Bullied

How difficult it must be for you,
To shield their poison arrows every day;
To feel so alone in a crowded school,
And have to live and learn that way.

To be teased about your weight,
By those, whose cruelty will not relent.
To watch your confidence melt away,
When you really only want a friend.

They have pushed you to the brink,
Where now, you've started to believe.
What they say is what you think,
And what you hoped may never be.

Listen to me son, hear what I say;
I know you better than anyone else.
I spent my youth in much the same way,
Don't ever lose faith in yourself.

You are a wonderful person inside;
So loving, so gentle and so smart.
You can accomplish whatever you try,
If you always listen to your heart.

They tease because they know the truth;
You have talents they will never know.
They have to work harder than you,
To make their progress even show.

They're jealous that you can go on,
Though they make your life so hard.
They know that what they do is wrong,
And they've taken it much too far.

Learn to laugh at the tricks they play,
Don't worry about trying to fit in.
Soon will come my son, a day,
That they will lose and watch you win

I'm so proud that you never retaliate,
Because you know you'd do them harm.
In life we must learn to negotiate,
With words, not the strength in our arms.

Their futures lay in dead end streets,
And homes broken by empty dreams.
Don't let them drag you down beneath,
No matter how futile these days seem.

You are a spark of life, yet to grow,
To the fullest height of your flame.
When you reach your lifetime goals,
They will remember you by name.

Your success will take them by surprise,
They'll wonder how you grew so strong.
But I will only look you in the eyes,
And say "I knew it all along"

The Victim

She lies there, snuggled in her warm bed;
A safari of stuffed animals to keep her safe.
There is a Sesami Street quilt covering her,
And a happy little smile on her face.

My beautiful little angel, deep in sleep;
Pleasant dreams she peacefully entertains.
Her youth is a sanctuary that protects her,
From Daddy's sudden loss and his pain.

My ambitious little Pokemon trainer,
So innocent, yet so full of energy and fire!
She will, no doubt achieve her goals;
She can be anything her little heart desires.

She is the glue that is holding together,
A family that has been torn in two.
Offering love when it is dearly needed,
And a hug when Daddy's feeling blue.

She is a tireless bundle of peace and joy;
A diplomat speaking wisely of her needs.
Trying to piece back together those she loves,
A stateswoman holding tightly to her dreams.

Her smile can move great mountains;
It can calm the most inclement weather.
She is so logical, not over swept with emotion;
She only wants her Mom and Dad together.

Why are we lost in this brutal disagreement,
Causing each other sadness and pain?
Why can't we be more like our little angel,
Trying so hard to show us both the way.

We are not the victims that we claim,
We are the aggressors instead.
The victim is that sweet little girl,
Lying there helpless, in her bed.

Boots

Where has my daughter gone, in such a hurry?
Why does her breakfast sit soggy and untouched?
Why has my son not turned on the TV I worry,
Until I find them both outside, playing with the new pup.

How often they had begged both their Mother and I,
And promised they would take care of their pet.
How could I see them with such want in their eyes,
For a friend they would love, and never neglect?

Their Mother was not as enthusiastic about it as I;
I had a wonderful dog on the day we first met.
She loved it immensely until the day that it died,
But she didn't like the yard to be in such a mess!

With my wife's departure, I wanted to calm the pain,
And the constant requests of my still pleading kids.
We went off to the dog pound with a collar and a chain,
To find a new friend; which is exactly what we did!

The abandoned little beagle, with it's long floppy ears,
Yelped for our attention from her steel covered cage.
It was more like a field mouse, or so it appeared,
For its tiny little body and its tender young age.

Our hearts were touched with that instant attraction,
And Boots came home to live with us in our house.
As time went swiftly past, we knew she was happy,
And I was released of my long standing doubts.

How priceless the love of a dog can be, for a family,
That has been torn in two by a recent separation.
The unconditional love that she offers for free,
Was a good cure for a heartbreaking situation.

We're all now stronger and Boots has taken her place,
In the family that has managed to keep upbeat.
As I look out in the yard, at my kids smiling faces,
I know that Boots is the best friend we could ever meet!

The Path of Life

When you walk your path in life,
Choose carefully your steps.
The road is full of traps and pitfalls.

Hold strangers within your sight.
Trusting no one will serve you best;
Always keep your back against the wall!

You can listen to their stories,
But never fall into their charms;
You must be wary of their words.

They may speak of guts and glory,
But may mean to do you harm,
Then leave you all alone and hurt.

There are some with good inside,
Who are sincere in their offers,
And can help you find your way.

Some truths can turn to lies,
When it isn't worth their bother,
And you question what they say.

Though some will walk beside you,
Don't depend on them to stay;
The road has far too many forks.

If you let their pace guide you,
You may just lose your way,
And never find your proper course.

Our lives are full of questions,
But the answers far and few;
No matter how we try to understand.

We are searchers of directions,
In most everything that we do,
And followers of other peoples plans.

Some are lucky; they find their way,
In the company of faithful friends;
They spend their lives complete.

Others fall and misery rules their days;
They suffer pain that never ends,
And their paths lead them to defeat.

How wonderful our journeys would be,
If we sought out our own goals,
And kept honesty in every stride.

If we all could harbour integrity,
In the deepest corners of our souls,
And hold love and goodwill inside.

How productive our efforts could be,
Without the potholes that dot our climb,
Through the travels that we undertake.

What beauty in life we all could see,
As we leave our youths behind,
And travel the road that yields our fates.

Love of Life and Nature:

What a beautiful world we have the pleasure of inhabiting!

There is nothing as wonderful as a nice ride in the country on an Autumn day, as nature paints the leaves a multitude of colours! What a majestic landscape; the first snow of the Winter as it covers up the dust and the dirt that a full year without it has accumulated; the numbness of the sudden cold and the preparation of nature to get ready to sleep until the Spring arrives. It's all so bleak until that first layer of snow reminds us that there is beauty at that time of year, at least until it all turns to slush and slop!

The season of Christmas comes upon us so quickly and with such a promising change in the hearts and the minds of men and women and especially in the children! It almost lets us forget the troubles of life, if only for a few weeks.

Just when we least expect it, the Spring air fills the skies and breathes into young men and women exciting thoughts of love. It's so pleasant to walk through the park with one eye on the flowers and the other on the magic of young love.

There is nothing like the warmth of the summer sun as we head towards the water to soak up its rays. There will always be the memories of being at the beach from the time we are young until the day that we are no longer able to find the time to get there. The trips to the cottage; the camping trips; hiking in the woods and sleeping under the stars!

There really is no aspect of this life that love does not touch. The seasons bring us close together to celebrate the holidays. We join together with family and friends that we love in order to catch up on what has happened since our last gathering. Every season has its own holiday or two that we take advantage of. The Summer family reunions, Thanksgiving, special days relative to the countries that we live in or the religions that we have chosen, of course Christmas and New Years as well.

There are joyous and even sad occasions that draw us together as well. Anniversaries, birthdays and graduations; funerals, Remembrance Day and tragic events that we never expected. We sometimes come to celebrate, but we also come to show support for those who have experienced hardship.

We are a species of loving people by nature, though we may not always show it. Life can make us change our views and turn us cold to those around us, but there is a little kid in all of us . We just have to let it out to play!

Spring

The last bit of Winters snow,
Trickles down the storm drain;
Stretching out its final breath.

Following its path, it knows,
It will linger, then return again,
Just when we least expect.

We venture outside together,
From our fossil fueled lairs,
Drawn by the warming sun.

We bask in the beautiful weather,
Though we all are aware,
That it may not yet have begun!

With reserved anticipation,
We step out onto our patios,
And gaze at the clear blue sky.

We stand still, in fascination,
As the crocuses that grow,
Push the melting snow aside.

Sand that swirls in the street,
Is proof of a Southern breeze;
We know we may just be right!

Lying there beneath our feet,
Autumns long forgotten leaves,
Exposed where they fell and died.

All of us inside, scream out a sigh,
Because Winter is finally gone.
The damn shovelling is finally through!

We dust off the summer toys;
Get ready to groom our lawns;
Wives make lists for husbands to do!

The gardeners prepare their soil,
With bags of peat moss spread,
Then forked into the clumpy land.

The sportsmen mix the gas and oil,
For the boat just out of the shed,
Holding tackle boxes in their hands!

Cottages, forgotten for the season,
Worry themselves into our thoughts;
Much like an old dying friend.

Their upkeep defies all reason,
But yet we disregard the costs,
And long to see them once again!

Garden hoses stretch for miles,
To the steel chariots we clean;
Our shop vacs all roar to life!

Collectors polish with a smile,
Their beloved muscle machines,
Until they glisten in the light.

Children flock into the streets,
With hockey sticks in hand,
And the playoffs looming near!

Teenagers find a shuffle in their feet;
Exciting changes they never planned,
Now that young love is in the air.

Of all of the seasons we observe,
Spring time affects us the most;
In peculiar, but magical ways.

The undressing of the Winter world,
Give us the reason for a toast,
To lift a drink for better days.

We take a good look at our lives,
As Spring rolls out at our feet
Like a green carpet from Gods hands.

Its beauty opens our eyes,
To the magic that lay silent beneath,
That dismal snow covered land.

Another wonder to be taken in,
Like the scent of a sweet rose;
Another year older, we venture out.

When the cold will come again,
We really never do know.
So we will enjoy Spring as it sprouts.

The Changing

The sullen quiet of the night,
Is pierced by a restless bullfrog,
Stirring ripples in the silent marsh.

In the last hours of moonlight,
I watch a half sunken, rotting log,
Bobbing along; following the dark.

Another day begins its untimely birth,
From the hollows of the fleeting night;
With the promises of what may be.

It sparks the re-awakening of the earth;
It tells us that things are still alright,
And calls to us to come and see.

It closes chapters within our minds,
That make their homes in our dreams,
And never seem to be complete.

It beckons us to leave behind,
The failures that we have seen,
As it lays a new chance at our feet.

The chorus of its warming rays,
Fill my ears with sounds of life,
As nature stirs its simmering pan.

The once calm water fills with waves,
As the wind proclaims its right,
To comb itself across the land.

Fatigue, the enforcer of my sleep,
Withdraws slowly in the light,
And retreats back to where it resides.

Sitting up in bed, I peel off the sheets,
That protected me from the night;
I rub my drowsy sleep drained eyes.

I think about the day before me,
To the whistle of my steaming kettle,
And the crunching of my teeth on toast.

My troubles waiting to receive me;
Standing firm and prepared for battle,
At the factory that I dread the most.

Outside my window, I see so clearly,
The thrashing of a taunting fish,
Daring me to come and try my luck.

The monster fish that I have so nearly,
Caught, to fill my dinner dish,
Teases me to cast my baited hook.

I curse the job that waits for me;
The boss that watches my every move,
With the eyes of a soaring hawk.

I swear that someday I will leave,
To live my life the way I choose,
And spring the trap in which I'm caught.

So many somedays have gone by,
Past my promise to free myself,
That my dream is wearing itself thin.

From these thoughts, I realize,
That time will never try to tell,
Unless you force it to begin.

The stroll towards my car pool,
Is diverted to the dock,
And the boat that awaits me there.

Those in the cattle car, think me a fool,
And they change their coffee talk;
A brand new gossip they can share.

Their exhaust trails up my lane,
And my motor roars its approval,
Re-assuring me of my daring choice.

My boss will think me quite insane,
And insist on my instant removal,
In his gruff and condescending voice.

On the water, I am one with the earth;
Seeking my prey with deep respect;
Knowing that I would set him free.

We both are creatures of our worth,
Set apart from the lives that we reject,
And proud of what we strive to be.

Seek your dreams in all that you do,
Don't be fearful that you may fall,
Or that your hopes are a waste of time.

Take the chance to see it through;
Heed your inner voice when it calls,
And never let them change your mind!

Lest We Forget

They lay in fields around the globe;
In shallow graves, unmarked.
In desperate times they left their homes,
With honour in their hearts.

Young men from their Mothers, torn;
Trained to fight and to defend.
In that rite, soon, soldiers born,
To wage a war that never ends.

Behind the rocks with rifles trained,
There is no time to remember,
The fields of corn and golden grain;
The pond rinks of December.

They stand alone beside their friends,
To the sounds of battle called.
They pray to God, but when it ends,
They watch their buddies fall.

Only luck will bring them home,
But luck can cost them limbs.
Those who fall will die alone,
It's the sacrifice it takes to win.

With freedom saved, the world goes on,
Until the next battle lies ahead.
Weary soldiers are the only ones,
That still pray for the dead.

As children play their video games,
Spraying bullets at a cyber scene;
There are no faces, nor any names,
Of the heroes who keep them free.

The wind sweeps the bloodied grass,
Stirring up the ashes from a rest alone.
Forgotten sacrifices of days long past;
The winds will finally bring them home.

On this day of cold winds in November,
Pin a poppy near your chest.
Your life is free, so please remember,
Lest we never shall forget.

Cry For the Victim

A cold granite monument,
In an empty December field;
Buried in snow; buried alive.

A long remembered testament,
To the dangers of solid steel,
In the hands of a drunken driver.

The tire marks have since faded.
The screech that filled the night,
Is over and all out of breath.

A family is forever separated,
By the fool who had no right,
To cause this tragic death.

After he sits there behind bars,
For a short moment in time;
The law grants him another chance.

Wash the blood from his car,
For he has paid for his crime;
Let's put the wheel back in his hands.

Out in that cold December field,
A family gathers to pay respects,
Outraged at society's lenience.

Lawyers and their business deals,
Twist the hollow laws we all elect;
They are mongers of incompetence.

The poor man was drunk that night,
How can we hold him to blame,
When alcohol was the ultimate cause?

The innocent child who lost his life,
Was run down in the pouring rain;
How can they justify the loss?

Cry for the victim, not the drunk who decided to drive.
With responsible decisions, they both would be alive.
Neither family would have hate or sorrow in their eyes.
So cry for the victim, not the damn fool that decided to drive.

Hay Bay

The cottage we own stands all alone,
In the cold North winds of a late Spring.
Our quiet, relaxing summer home,
Is denied an early opening!

The sunshine sparkles through the cold;
Luring us into a hope for change.
The weather mans predictions told,
Not too good for the next few days.

Though the Winter snow is finally gone,
And the grass turns a greenish hue;
The coldness seems to linger on,
So waiting is the only thing we can do.

There just isn't enough summer in life,
To do the things we most like to do.
Once the work is done, we've run out of time,
And summer seems to slip right through.

We take on projects we needlessly invent,
And make improvements that aren't required.
We work, then work harder without relent,
Until suddenly our Summer has expired.

All Winter we think about resting and relaxing,
With nothing to do but to fish and to swim.
We will never admit that a cottage is taxing,
And the work it involves seems to never end.

By the end of the summer, numb to the bone,
We are just about ready to call it a season.
Believe it or not, we look forward to home,
Where we can finally relax for no reason.

Once again, the cottage we own stands all alone,
In the cold North winds of a late Spring.
The cycle repeats with our moans and our groans;
We can't wait for the work to begin!

Christmas Eve

Coloured baubles hang on pine boughs,
Glistening in the dim evening light;
Outside, the scraping of snow ploughs,
Pierce the silence of this special night.

Stockings, tacked to the fireplace mantle,
Wait to be filled with candies and toys.
Wide eyed children, waiting for Santa,
Try hard to be good little girls and boys.

Packages wrapped and trimmed in bows,
Are scattered everywhere under the tree.
Grandfathers speak about Christmases of old;
The youngest child still awake on his knee.

Shortbread cookies, meat pies and cakes,
Will very soon be ready to be shared.
The last batch of cookies is finally baked,
And the turkey is trimmed and prepared.

The last Childs eyes droop and then close;
And is tucked with a kiss, safely off to sleep.
The adults pour drinks and offer a toast,
As they sit down, finally resting their feet.

In the distance, so loud and clear;
The clanging of the churches last bells.
Midnight mass is over and Christmas is here,
And for one day, our entire world is well.

Christmas is Coming

Sleigh tracks through the fresh snow,
Criss-crossing through the fields;
The laughter of children as they play.

Smiling faces everywhere you go;
That sense of peace that we all show,
Realizing it will soon be Christmas Day.

Santa line-ups at the local mall,
Full of kids with letters clutched in hand;
Waiting impatiently to have their say.

Giant snowflakes start to fall,
Spreading a white blanket on the land;
It won't be long until Christmas Day!

Shoppers hustle from store to store,
Banging and clanging their shopping carts;
Trying to get it done and out of the way.

Frustrated, they can't take it anymore,
But they keep the kindness in their hearts,
Because tomorrow is finally Christmas Day!

Tiny kids, too wide eyed to fall asleep;
Feeling the magic that comes with daylight,
And the new toys with which they will soon play.

Peace on earth in this tiny little Town,
Is followed with another sprinkling of snow,
That comes dramatically and with no warning.

Sleigh tracks on the freshly christened ground,
Beat a path to church where we all will go,
On this very wondrous Christmas morning.

Tragic Peaceful Night

There's something in the air, something magic;
Something in the eyes of everyone today.
The year has been so hectic, so often tragic;
But all of that will change on Christmas Day.

We'll share our time with families and friends,
And eat turkey until our bellies are far too full.
Expensive gifts will pass from hand to hand;
The love that's shown will warm the Winter chills.

All of the suffering and the social injustices;
Will be forgotten while the home fires burn.
It will still be there, waiting to re-surface,
When this special day is over and reality returns.

Those who're alone, with no-one to share their lives;
Those without a blanket to keep them warm;
Those who watch their children starve and die,
Unsheltered from this society's violent storms.

The abused, the neglected and the mentally ill;
The sick, the political prisoners and the weak.
While there is joy and contentment on the hill,
There is sorrow and sadness on the streets.

Let's not forget the pure thought of the day;
Try to remember what peace on earth is all about.
Dig deeper; don't let contentment steal away,
The opportunity to help another human out.

Feed the hungry; lay a blanket at their feet;
Give a child a gift that may keep them alive.
Offer shelter to those who will surely freeze;
Send a beacon out, on this very special night.

Christmas can truly be a very wondrous day,
If we share with those who rely on us to care.
The peace we feel inside will never go away,
And the happiness will spread to everywhere.

On this Holiest of nights, keep it in your mind;
It's our duty to give help to others every day.
Don't leave the sorrows of the earth behind;
One day of peace won't take those pains away.

A Lonely Christmas

The seasons have turned so fast,
But some things never seem to change.
Summer is gone and Autumn has passed,
And Christmas is upon us again.

The children are crazy with anticipation;
Advent calendars open one tag at a time.
Parents are coming to the realization,
That credit card interest rates are a crime.

The tree is decorated, the mistletoe hung;
The lights are strung across the front deck.
The songbooks are there, ready to be sung,
And I am nothing but a nervous wreck!

So much going on around me at home;
Everyone laughing and sharing hugs.
My heart is spending this Christmas alone,
Because sometimes family just isn't enough.

If you ask me what I would like to see,
It would lead me to say that it's you;
Wrapped up in a bow beside my tree,
You would make my wishes come true.

Christmas is almost here, it won't be long;
It reminds me of Christmases from my past.
Some so great but some so terribly wrong;
The bad ones never fade too fast.

This year my thoughts will be of you,
Still far away though, wherever you may be.
I will do my best to smile and get through,
What will be a very lonely Christmas for me

To A Mother

With all of my heart,
I want to share with you,
The love that I have inside.
You've been a huge part of me,
And the things that I do,
For every minute of my life.

Whenever I am sick,
You try to comfort me,
And nurse me back to health.
My skin can be thick,
But you are patient with me,
And you teach me love as well.

I don't have the words to say,
How deeply I love you Mom;
But I have the courage to try.
I will cherish you in every way,
From the day my life was begun,
Until that final day I die.

I will hold you as my friend,
In my heart and my soul;
The shiniest jewel in my life.
I know I always can depend,
On a loving hand to hold,
On the loneliest of nights.

I guess what I am trying to say,
In a way you'll understand,
Is that I will love you forever.
On this special Christmas Day,
The best part of our plans,
Is for us to be together!

Fifty Years

A lifetime of respect;
A journey that was shared,
With love as the foundation.
Fifty years together,
For two lovers who cared,
To reach that destination.

A silence between them;
The words " I love you ",
Is spoken in their eyes.
That long ago dream,
They hoped would come true,
Has now been realized!

Many smiles; a few tears;
But at the end of the day,
A sweet kiss goodnight.
In the passage of fifty years,
It has remained that way,
At each others sides.

A treasure to behold;
These days, so rarely seen,
To have lived it through together.
More valuable than gold,
Is the fruition of your dreams,
Being hand and hand forever.

Congratulations and thank you,
For showing us all your love,
And your courage and respect.
May this Anniversary of fifty years,
Be one of many more to come!
We wish you all the best!

In Conclusion:

It is my sincerest hope that you have enjoyed this little journey through the positives and the negatives of love. I realize that these are only my interpretations of the experiences that love has seen fit to offer me and that every person is different and the joys and sorrows that they have endured are different as well. Similar perhaps, but certainly not the same!

As I see it, the bottom line is that love is worth the effort despite the roller coaster ride that it presents to us. Where would we be in this life without it? I'm sure that the good times really do outweigh the bad and I think if we examine it, we can all come to that conclusion.

It's the pain of the breakup that makes it so intensely sad for us. Strangely enough, it's human nature to remember the bad times more clearly and more distinctly than the good ones. That in itself, is the greatest tragedy of falling out of love.

My hope is that in your experiences, there were and are at least enough happy times that if you need to walk away, at least you can walk away with some sort of reward. We really do have to look for positives in this life as opposed to finding the ever present negatives. They are out there and they can be found!

Anyone and everyone that has been a part of my life and my love, I hope that you have found what was not possible for us to locate together. I hold no grudges, no animosity and certainly, at this point in my life, no regrets. I very much hope that it's the same for you.

To those still looking, I wish you the very best of luck in your search. Stay strong, stay focused and stick to your guns when you have the opportunity for romance. Don't compromise your expectations or your morals and beliefs. If it is meant to be, then it will be! If it isn't this one, then it may well be the next.

To those who have managed to keep their love fresh and alive through the years, I offer congratulations. I'm sure you both know how precious your love is and how many others can only dream of finding what you already have. I know that it requires a lot of give and take over the years . . . I saw it first hand with my parents.
It's a proud and monumental accomplishment that not many can lay claim to!

To those who may be in a bad situation in their relationship; who may not have the clear presence of mind to see it for what it really is ... please find the help that you need to walk away from it. It may seem impossible, but if there is abuse in your household then you owe it to yourself, your spouse and to your children to put an end to that horrible cycle that has trapped you within. Life will get better if you take that ever important first step.

To all of you in love or out, God Bless

William G. Ferguson